Gimp
Pocket Reference

Sven Neumann

Translated by Sven Riedel

Beijing • Cambridge • Farnham • Köln • Sebastopol • Tokyo

Gimp Pocket Reference

by Sven Neumann, translated by Sven Reidel

Copyright © 2000 O'Reilly Media, Inc. All rights reserved. Printed in the United States of America.

Published by O'Reilly Media, Inc., 101 Morris Street, Sebastopol, CA 95472.

Editor: Chuck Toporek

Production Editor: Sarah Jane Shangraw

Cover Designer: Hanna Dyer

Printing History:

March 1999:	First Edition, German Language Edition (*Gimp kurz & gut*)
August 2000:	Second Edition, German Language Edition (*Gimp kurz & gut*)
September 2000:	First Edition, English Language Edition

Library of Congress Cataloging-in-Publication Data is available at: *http://www.ora.com/catalog/gimppr/*.

ISBN: 978-1-565-92731-5
[LSI] [2011-08-12]

Table of Contents

Gimp Pocket Reference

Introduction

The GNU Image Manipulation Program, or *Gimp*, is a powerful and complex Open Source image editing program. Because the Gimp's ability can be expanded with plug-ins and scripts, its functionally is virtually limitless. This reference will introduce you to version 1.2 of the Gimp and all the plug-ins and scripts that are part of the standard distribution. This book will help the novice, who wants to learn about the Gimp's features, as well as the experienced user who wants to look up certain functions. Some effort has been put to the task to document the many, sometimes hidden, features that make working with the Gimp more efficient.

Structure and Conventions

This reference starts with a description of the Toolbox, the Gimp's main window, and the functions that can be accessed from here. The second section of this Pocket Reference deals with the Image window and the functions reached through the Context menu that can be opened by right-clicking in any image window. We will closely follow the Context menu's hierarchy, making it fast and easy for you to look up specific functions. References to other menu items in the text will follow this structure as well. For example, *<Image>Filters* points to the *Filters* menu inside the *Image* menu. The Toolbox also contains a menu hierarchy that provides access to functions that do not apply to any specific image. Since some functions are accessible only via the Extensions menu, we will also use the *<Toolbox>Xtns* notation where appropriate.

The standard shortcut key of a function is in parenthesis next to its description—for example, *Quit (CTRL-Q)*. See *"Creating and Editing Keyboard Shortcuts"* to learn how to define your own keyboard shortcuts.

This book also covers the Gimp's use of some not-so-common Perl modules. If these Perl modules are not installed on your system, you won't be able to use some of the functions that Perl adds to the Gimp. Functions that require the use of Perl have been marked with a Camel icon.

Understanding the Gimp, and image manipulation in general, requires an understanding of some technical terms. These terms are explained in the Appendix, along with a list of the image file formats, and their respective properties, that the Gimp can handle.

The Toolbox

The Toolbox, as illustrated in Figure 1, is the Gimp's main window. This first section of this book describes the functions accessible through the Toolbox's menus, its tools, and finally, the color-selector and preview areas located at the bottom of the Toolbox. The Toolbox may be resized to whatever shape you like by simply dragging its borders with the mouse.

File

The Gimp has two different File menus, one located in the Toolbox, and the other in the Image window. The Toolbox's File menu (*<Toolbox>File*) contains only those functions specific to an image, in addition to an image history, which offers easy access to images on which you have recently worked. Each image also has its own File menu (*<Image>File*), with options that allow you to save and print images. These options include:

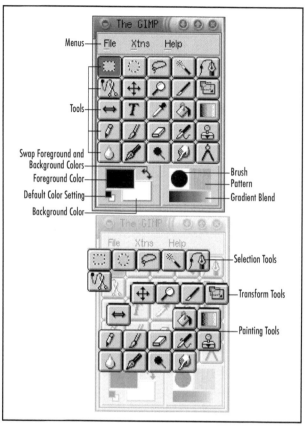

Menus
Tools
Swap Foreground and Background Colors
Foreground Color
Default Color Setting
Background Color
Brush
Pattern
Gradient Blend
Selection Tools
Transform Tools
Painting Tools

Figure 1. At the heart of the Gimp is the Toolbox, offering a variety of tools for image manipulation and design.

New (CTRL-N)

Creates a new image. If invoked from the Toolbox, the values for the last image created in this session (e.g., image type and size), are used as the default values. (Default image values can be set with *<Toolbox>*

File→Preferences.) *<Image>File→New* copies the properties from the current image and applies them to a new image editing window.

Open (CTRL-O)

Loads an image from disk. The Open dialog can do command-line completion (i.e., pressing the TAB key will complete the filename if there are no ambiguities). Hidden files and directories are not displayed in the dialog, but can be directly accessed by entering their names. Pressing SHIFT or CTRL while selecting the filenames allows you to open multiple images at the same time. Shift-clicking allows you to select a range of images in a directory, while Control-clicking allows you to select specific files.

Saving an image will also create and save a small preview of the image. The Gimp uses the same file format for the preview that the program *xv* uses for its own previews. This preview is displayed in the file list. Clicking the preview will cause an up-to-date preview of the image to be generated. If all of the files in the list have been selected and the preview area is clicked, previews will be generated for each image.

The Gimp recognizes the image by reading the first few bytes of data (the file format's "magic number"). If The Gimp fails to identify the image type, it will try to do so based on its file extension. If you want to load a valid image file whose extension is not correct, the file type can be set manually by selecting it from the *Determine File Type* menu. Compressed files with the *.gz* or *.bz2* extensions are decompressed automatically when opened if the *gunzip* or *bunzip2* programs are installed on your system.

Acquire

Plug-ins that load images from some place other than the hard disk (e.g., scanners) are placed here. *Xsane*, a Unix front-end for the *SANE* scanner library, cooperates especially well with the Gimp. The Windows version of the Gimp has a plug-in that can communicate with scanners via the TWAIN interface.

Screen Shot

A front-end to the *xwd* program in the Unix version of the Gimp; a separate plug-in is available for the Windows version. A single window, with or without window manager decorations (e.g., title bar or window frames) or the entire desktop can be the focus of the screenshot. If a single window is to be dumped, the cursor will change to a cross after the GRAB button is pushed; the screenshot of the desired window can be grabbed by simply clicking it.

Preferences

Offers configuration options for Gimp internals and the GUI. The settings are described later in the "Preferences" section.

Dialogs

Gives access to a number of dialogs, which are covered later in the "Dialogs" section.

Quit (CTRL-Q)

Quits the Gimp. If any image has not been saved since its last change, the Gimp will ask you whether you want to quit without saving changes.

Xtns (Gimp Extensions)

Gimps extensions are accessible though the Toolbox's Xtns menu. Most functions found in the Xtns menu are plug-ins or scripts which are, in contrast to the filters found in the Image menu, not associated with a specific image. The extensions include:

Module Browser

Some functions of the GIMP are implemented as modules (e.g., the color selection dialog). The *Module Browser* displays a list of all loaded modules and offers the ability to inhibit the automatic loading of modules, which can save launching time and memory.

DB Browser

The Gimp places its internal functions in a *Procedural Database* (PDB), allowing them to be called by plug-ins and scripts. Furthermore, each plug-in and script adds its own calling function to the database so they can execute each other. The *DB Browser* displays the functions that have been added to the PDB, as well as their input and output parameters.

PDB Explorer 🐪

An alternative to the *DB Browser*, written in Perl.

Plug-in Details

Displays a list of all available plug-ins, which can be searched for by name. This is a nice feature to use when you can't remember where a certain plug-in resides in the menu hierarchy.

Parasite Editor 🐪

The Gimp uses parasites to save plug-in settings, either globally or on a per-image basis. This editor offers access to the parasites, although you shouldn't have to edit anything in this dialog.

Unit Editor

The Unit Editor offers an easy way to modify the *unitrc* file. If your favorite unit (e.g., furlongs or fathoms) is not yet present, you can add it to the Gimp using the Unit Editor.

Perl 🐪

Since version 1.0, the Gimp's support of scripting languages has expanded from the original "Script-Fu" to include *Python* and *Perl*. The Perl menu allows access to the Perl Control Center (PCC), which contains information about the Perl installation and a *logfile* of error messages. The Perl Server, which lets external Perl scripts control the Gimp remotely, is launched from here as well.

Render 🐫

> This menu includes some scripts that generate logos or nice effects. All functions in this menu are implemented in Perl.

Script-Fu

> In addition to a whole slew of web-graphic and logo scripts, this menu contains the *Script-Fu Console*. Here, you can enter Script-Fu commands (Script-Fu is a Scheme dialect). *REFRESH*ing will make the Gimp re-read scripts, enabling scripts and changes to be added without having to restart the Gimp.

Split Video to Frames

> The same menu as found under *<Image>Video*.

Web Browser

> If the Netscape browser is installed on your system, the Web Browser menu offers direct links to a variety of web pages on the official Gimp web site (*http://www.gimp.org/*), and to other Gimp-related sites on the Internet.

Help

The Gimp has a built-in help system that can be accessed from the Toolbox (*<Toolbox>Help*), or by pressing *F1*. It's important to note, however, that the Gimp's help system is incomplete. It includes:

Help (F1)

> Opens the Gimp's help browser.

Context Help (SHIFT-F1)

> Changes the cursor to a question mark. Point and click on an icon or GUI element and the help browser will open and tell you about its use.

Tip of the Day

> Shows the *Tip of the Day*. Going through these tips once is definitely worth the effort.

About
> Shows the version of your Gimp installation and lists the names of its developers.

Tools

The Gimp's tools are displayed as icons in the Toolbox. Clicking an icon will select the corresponding tool. Double-clicking the icon will open an option window for that particular tool.

This section lists the Gimp's tools in the same order as they appear in the Toolbox, starting with the upper-left button, the Rectangular Selection tool. Functions that are hidden in some menus can be regarded as tools; these will be explained in the section corresponding to their position in the menu structure and are marked by an icon next to their name.

If a tool's function is invoked by dragging the mouse (with the exception of the drawing tools), it may be canceled even before the function takes effect by pressing and holding down the right mouse button while releasing the left mouse button.

Selection Tools

Selection tools are important utilities in image manipulation. They are used to define selection masks (a marked area), upon which functions can be applied exclusively. The Gimp marks the border of a selection with an animated dashed line. A selection doesn't necessarily require a clearly defined border. You can also have the border of the selection fade out softly. This is done by using the *Feather Radius* option, which is common to all selection tools. Feathered selections display border markers with pixels reduced by 50 percent. Another tool option available with all selection tools is *Antialiasing,* which eliminates the staircase effect at the selection's border.

A selection, along with its contents, can by moved by dragging it with the mouse. This will implicitly convert the selection into a floating selection. To move the border of a selection without its contents, press ALT while dragging the mouse.*

Selection tools usually create a new selection, but it is possible to combine the new selection with an existing one. The mode of combination depends on which key is being held down when the mouse button is pressed, as outlined in Table 1 which shows the Keyboard-click combinations.

Table 1. Keyboard-click combinations

Key	Action
SHIFT	Addition
CTRL	Subtraction
SHIFT + CTRL	Intersection

<Image>SelectByColor menu item provides an additional means of selecting a region, but it is not covered in the following list, since it is not present in the Toolbox. This tool selects areas based upon their color (see *Select by Color*).

Rect Select (R) and Ellipse Select (E)

These tools create rectangular and elliptical selections, and behave very similarly. Dragging creates a selection, which is fixed once you release the mouse button. To deselect a selection, just click outside of the selected area, on the canvas.

---

* If the Image window moves instead of the selection, your window manager reserves the ALT key for itself. In this case, you should reconfigure your window manager so that it frees the ALT key for the Gimp.

The CTRL and SHIFT keys add an additional function to these tools. While holding down the key with the mouse button being pressed, you can determine the way the current selection and an existing one are combined. The key that is pressed down when the mouse button is released determines the geometry of the new selection. Table 2 shows the keyboard-click/release combinations for the rectangular and elliptical selection tools.

Table 2. Keyboard-click/release combinations

Key	Before mouse button	After mouse button
SHIFT	Addition	Square or circle.
CTRL	Subtraction	Origin defines the center.
SHIFT + CTRL	Intersection	Square or circle around the center.

These functions can be used in any combination. For example, imagine you want to cut a circle out of an existing rectangular selection. To do this, use the elliptical selection tool (E) and place the cursor over the of the existing rectangular selection. Hold down the CTRL key while pressing the mouse button, then press and hold SHIFT+CTRL while dragging the mouse and releasing the mouse button. The selection is now a fixed elliptical area centered on the rectangle.

Fixed Size/Aspect Ratio
   Creates a selection with a fixed size. Pressing SHIFT while creating the selection creates a selection with variable size, but with a fixed aspect ratio.

Free Select (F)

Use this tool to select an area by tracing an outline with the mouse. When the mouse button is released, the selection is closed by joining the starting and ending points with a straight line.

Fuzzy Select (Z)

The Fuzzy Select tool or "magic wand" selects a contiguous area around the indicated pixel. Neighboring pixels with a similar color to that of the selected pixel are included in the selection. The color threshold can be set in the *Threshold* option or by dragging the mouse while the mouse button is being held down.

Sample Merged

Takes the colors of other layers into account, if these are visible.

Threshold

Sets the maximum deviation allowed for a pixel to be included in the selection region.

Bezier Selection (B)

This tool creates and manipulates paths. Paths are implemented as bezier curves with control points, offering the ability to edit the tangent of a curve at each point. To create a bezier selection, you first need to define the curve's vertices. This is done by clicking the canvas. After closing the path by placing the final vertex on top of the first, you can edit the vertices and connect lines of the curve. To edit a point, select it by clicking on it. You can change the tangent at this point by dragging the mouse. Pressing SHIFT will allow you to edit more than one connecting line at a time. Dragging the mouse with CTRL held down moves the vertice freely around the canvas. To select a curve, click into the area enclosed by the curve. The Paths dialog (see *Layers, Channels and Paths*) contains a list of the currently available paths and offers a set of tools with which the paths may be further manipulated.

Any selection can be converted to a path by selecting *<Image>Selec→To Path*, which makes paths powerful tools for manipulating selections.

Intelligent Scissors (I)

While almost useless in version 1.0, Intelligent Scissors has become a very powerful tool for selecting complex image contents. Clicking on an image sets control points, and the Gimp will try to connect them by finding and following strong contrasts in the image. Any control point besides the starting or ending point can be moved by clicking and dragging it to a new position. The area that is to be selected is closed by placing a final control point on top of the first one; after this, you may select an area by clicking into it.

Transform Tools

Possible transformations include moving, rotation, flipping, and magnifying. The GIMP's tools for performing such transformations follow.

 Move Tool (M)

With the Move tool, an entire layer or an existing floating can be moved by simply dragging it with the mouse. The layer which has a visible pixel at the cursor's current position is moved. This allows picture elements to be moved intuitively. You can force the active layer to be moved by pressing SHIFT while clicking the mouse button, even if it does not contain opaque pixels at the given position.

You can also use the cursor keys to position layers. Press Cursor key to move a pixel in a given direction. Press SHIFT while using the cursor keys to move the layer in 25-pixel increments.

The Move tool can also be used to create and position guide lines. To create a guide, click on the rulers at the top or right of the Image window. This will automatically select the Move tool. Now you can drag a guide onto the image. Use the Move tool to reposition the guides in the image. To delete guides, simply drag them back onto the ruler. Guides can be set precisely with the Measure tool (see *Drawing Tools*).

Magnify Tool (SHIFT-M)

The Magnify tool changes the magnification level of the image display. Select the area to zoom into by dragging the mouse. Simply clicking onto the image will zoom in at the given point by one magnification step; CTRL and click will zoom out. The Gimp can display magnification levels in the range of 1:16 to 16:1. If the *Dot for Dot* option is enabled a zoom level of 1:1 means that one image pixel corresponds to one pixel on your screen. Otherwise, the image is displayed with the correct length and height (assuming that you specified your monitor resolution in the Preferences; see *The Preferences Dialog*). Some accelerator keys have been defined for the zoom tool (see "View").

Allow Window Resizing
   Adjusts the window to fit the zoomed image, if possible.

Tool Toggle
   Toggles between zooming in and out, using the CTRL key.

Crop & Resize (SHIFT-C)

This tool can be used to resize the image or a single layer.

Select an area by dragging the mouse. The area will be surrounded by a frame. The top-left and bottom-right corners of the frame can be used for resizing, while the other two corners will reposition the frame. Depending on the status of the *Allow Enlarging* option, the edges of the frame are either limited to the image area, or may extend beyond the image borders. This option can be toggled by pressing the ALT key.

The exact position and dimensions of the frame can be set in the dialog window that appears as soon as this tool is

---

used. Clicking on the *From Selection* button in this dialog box will adjust the frame to fit an existing selection or, if no selection exists, the entire image.

The *Auto Shrink* function works in a similar way to *Autocrop*; it will shrink a selected area automatically, until the colors at the edges of the selected area differ. This enables a precise selection of free floating picture elements.

Clicking inside the selected area will crop the image; every part of the image (or, if *Current Layer Only* has been selected, the current layer) outside the frame is discarded unless *Resize* has been selected. If *Resize* has been selected, the parts outside the frame are not thrown away; they are kept and can be made visible again with another *Resize*. This option can be toggled with the CTRL key.

Current Layer Only
>   This will perform the action only on the current layer, instead of on the entire image.

Allow Enlarging
>   Allows the crop frame to enlarge beyond the borders of the image (ALT).

Tool Toggle
>   Toggles between *Crop* and *Resize* (CTRL).

🖳 Transform Tool (SHIFT-T)

The Options dialog offers four different transformations:

Rotation
>   Rotates the current active layer or selection. The rotation angle is set by dragging the mouse. Holding down CTRL will force the angle to be a multiple of 15. Rotations by multiples of 90 degrees are performed faster by using the corresponding function from the *<Image>Layers* or *<Image>Image→Transforms* menu.

Scaling

For free scaling. Holding down SHIFT will allow you to scale only vertically. Use CTRL to scale only horizontally. Holding down both SHIFT and CTRL will maintain the image's aspect ratio during scaling.

Shearing

For shearing a selection or the active layer. Shearing will transform a rectangle into a parallelogram. The direction of the first mouse movement will determine if the shearing will be done horizontally or vertically.

Perspective

The most general of the transformation tools. This function allows you to distort the image's perspective by dragging the corners of an overlaid mesh.

The transformation can be done in two different ways. If *Tool Paradigm Traditional* was selected, the mesh describes the image after the transformation. On the other hand, if *Corrective* mode was used, the transformation works the other way around—the mesh indicates which image lines will be horizontal or vertical after the function was applied. This mode is especially useful for correcting slightly rotated scans or perspective distortions in photos. The result of a *Corrective* transformation can be much bigger than the original. In this case, the *Clip Result* option will crop parts that go beyond image boundaries.

All transformation functions are very CPU-intensive. Larger images will take a while to transform, so either be prepared for a coffee break, or turn *Smoothing* off.

If the image contains locked paths (indicated by a small padlock to the left of the path preview—see *Path Dialog*), the paths are transformed along with the image.

Tool Paradigm
    Determines how the transformation is to be applied.

Smoothing
    Considerably enhances the quality of the transformation
    result.

Clip Result
    Crops the image to the original image boundaries after
    the transformation.

Show Path
    Displays the paths, if they are locked (see *Path Dialog*).

⟷ Flip Tool (SHIFT-F)

Flips the selection of the active layer. You can choose the
direction of the flip in the Options dialog, or by toggling
this setting with the CTRL key.

Tool Toggle
    Toggles between horizontal and vertical flipping by
    using the CTRL key.

T Text Tool (T)

Inserts text into an image. Clicking the image after selecting this tool will open the text dialog. Here you can choose
a font from those that are offered by the X server, select its
size, and enter the text. Multirow text has to be entered one
row at a time, as the Gimp does not yet support text in
multiple rows. The text is inserted into the image as a floating selection and should be converted to a layer to make
subsequent corrections easier. Multirow text has to be
entered either by repeated use of the text tool, or by using
the *Dynamic Text* plug-in (see *Dynamic Text*), which
allows you to edit text after it has been rendered.

Antialiasing

Prevents staircase effects at diagonal lines. This is done by calculating the text for three times the given size and scaling it back down.

Border

Creates a border of the given pixel size around the text. This border is not visible—it just enlarges the text layer. This can be useful if the text is to be manipulated (e.g., blurred) afterward.

NOTE

The Gimp has a tendency to crop some italic fonts. Actually, this is a bug in the X server that returns incorrect font sizes. *Border* can help by defining the shape of the text.

Use Dynamic Text

Invokes the Dynamic Text plug-in instead of the standard text tool.

Color Picker (O)

The foreground color is set to the hue of the selected pixel. A pop-up window displays information about the color composition and the color's hexadecimal code, for use in HTML (e.g., #000C78 or #FFCC00).

Sample Merged

This option uses the color that is actually seen. This color may be created by overlapping several layers with different colors.

Sample Average

Returns the average color over an area.

Update Active Color

Copies the selected color to the currently active color in the Toolbox (either the fore- or background color, whichever is selected in the Toolbox).

Paint Tools

The Gimp's drawing tools use the active brush, which can be set in the Brush dialog (*<Image>Dialogs→Brushes*) or by clicking the brush preview in the Toolbox. The brush determines the shape and size of the applied color. The *Global Paint Options* (see "Preferences") determine if the opacity and mode of applying the color canvas (see "Color Models") is the same for all drawing tools. If the option is active, *Opacity* and *Mode* are associated with the brush and can be set in the Brush dialog. Otherwise, they, can be set individually for each drawing tool in the tool's Options dialog.

All drawing tools let you draw straight lines: Pressing SHIFT and clicking the mouse will draw a straight line to the last place the tool touched the canvas.

If you are using a graphic tablet with a pressure-sensitive pen, you might be interested in the pressure information options that some tools offer. *Pressure Sensitivity* options can be combined in any given way; however, not all tools offer all of the following options:

Opacity:
Controls the opacity of the color applied.

Pressure:
Makes the brush act as if it were harder or softer.

Rate:
Influences the setting rate of the active tool. It does not work with all tools.

Size:
Changes the size of the brush.

Color:
Uses a color from the current gradient instead of the foreground color. The pressure determines the position at which the color is taken from the gradient.

If pressure sensitive input devices are not used (or not configured, see "Input Devices" in the *Palette* section), these settings will have no effect.

Bucket Fill (SHIFT-B)

Color is poured into the selected position, spreading until it meets pixels whose color difference to the selected pixel surpasses a given threshold. If a selection exists, the whole selection is filled. To fill an entire layer, select it first (CTRL-A). A much faster way to achieve this is to drag and drop the color from any color field (e.g., fore- or background color in the Toolbox) into the selection.

Threshold
Specifies a threshold at which the color flow will stop.

Sample Merged
While only the color of the pixel in the active layer is normally considered, this option uses the color that is actually seen. This color may be composed of several different layered colors.

Fill Type
Either the foreground color is used (*Color Fill*), or the currently selected pattern (*Pattern Fill*). CTRL toggles the used color between fore- and background color.

Blend (L) Introduces a gradient color to the image. Dragging the mouse will set starting and ending points. Pressing CTRL while dragging will force the angle between the starting and ending point to be a multiple of 15 degrees. A color gradient will be created along the connecting line. This tool has many options, which can be discovered by experimenting and trying out different combinations.

Opacity
Controls the overall opacity of the gradient, from transparent to completely opaque.

Tools

Offset

The offset indicates the distance from the starting coordinate at which the blend should actually begin. It is expressed as a number in the range 0 to 100 that describes a proportionate distance between the starting and ending coordinates.

Blend

There are a few ways to blend colors:

FG to BG (RGB)

Blends from foreground to background color through RGB color space.

FG to BG (HSV)

Blends from foreground to background color through HSV color space. Creates rainbow-like gradients.

FG to Transparent

Blends from foreground color to transparency.

Custom Gradient

Uses the active gradient from the gradient editor (*<Image>Dialogs→Gradient Editor*).

Gradient

There are a few types of gradients:

Linear

Along the line from the starting to the ending point.

Bi-linear

Along the line from the starting point to the middle and from there to the ending point with reverse orientation.

Radial

A circular blend. The starting point defines the center of the circle; the ending point the radius.

Square

A square blend. The starting point defines the center or the square; the ending point is considered to be on the edge.

Conical

Blending around the starting point in a circle. Either once around (*Asymmetric* option) or back and forth (*Symmetric* option).

Shapeburst

Starting and ending points are not defined. According to the shape of the active selection, a three-dimensional effect is created. The *Angular*, *Spherical* and *Dimpled* options set the smoothness of the implied body.

Spiral

A spiral blend around the starting point, which is interpreted as the center point of the blend. The spiral will either be created with a *Clockwise* or *Anti-clockwise* (counter-clockwise) rotation. The distance between starting and ending points determines how dense the spiral is.

Repeat

Determines how the gradient will be repeated beyond the bounding points.

None

No repetitions. The color remains constant beyond the bounding points.

Sawtooth Wave

The gradient is repeated with the same orientation.

Triangular Wave

The gradient is repeated with alternating orientations.

Adaptive Supersampling

Significantly enhances the quality of the gradient, but uses more CPU time.

Pencil (SHIFT-P)

The pencil has a hard tip, applying color with full force over all of the brushed surface. This means that even if the

---

brush has a soft fading edge, the edges of the drawn lines will still be hard. The pencil is useful for drawing fine contours and editing single pixels.

Incremental

This will have an effect only if a brush with semi-transparent pixels is used. The opacity of the applied color increases each time the brush passes over an area.

 Paintbrush (P)

The Paintbrush will draw exactly the way the brush is shown in the dialog. Diagonal lines do not have the aliasing effect because of the smooth edges of the brush. Thin, straight lines usually seem to be too worn out; the pencil is a better tool for creating these.

Incremental

If the same area is repeatedly painted over, Incremental increases the opacity of the painted colors. Works with semi-transparent brushes only.

Fade Out

Fades the paintbrush during the drawing, as if it were running out of paint. The value determines how long the color will last. This option is disabled with a value of zero (0).

Gradient

Takes the color from the currently active gradient, as shown in the Toolbox. Different modes of application can be specified in the menu:

Once Forward

Uses all colors from the gradient from start to finish exactly once.

Once Backward

Does the same thing as Once Forward, only from back to front.

Loop Sawtooth
> Once the Paintbrush reaches the final color, it will start using colors from the front again.

Loop Triangle
> Will continuously go through the gradient from front to back to front again. The length of the gradient can be entered in the input field for this option.

 Eraser (SHIFT-E)

The Eraser will make pixels transparent, or, if it is used on a layer without alpha channel, the pixels will turn to the current background color instead.

Incremental
> If the same area is repeatedly painted over, *Incremental* increases the transparency of the pixels. This option works with semi-transparent pixels only.

Hard Edge
> Gives the eraser a hard edge, like a pencil.

Anti Erase
> This option has an effect only in layers with an alpha channel. It applies the eraser effect backward—instead of adding transparency to erased pixels, it makes them more opaque. This setting can be toggled with CTRL.

 Airbrush (A)

The airbrush applies color gradually. The longer the airbrush remains at the same place, the more color applied at this position, and the bigger the color splotch.

Incremental
> If the same area is repeatedly painted over, the *Incremental* option increases the transparency of the pixels with each pass. This works with semi-transparent pixels only.

Rate

Gives the amount of color applied per time unit. Low values result in smooth lines, high values show unsteady spray effects.

Pressure

Determines how much color is applied in the first moment this tool is used.

 ## Clone (C)

This tool is used to copy an area of an image; after selecting an image area as a source, this part of the image can be applied to a different area using the brush. The source is selected by clicking the desired position while holding down CTRL. During cloning, a small cross shows the current position from which image parts are copied. Source and destination do not have to be in the same image. For example, you can clone a section from any image into another.

Source

If *Pattern Source* is selected instead of an image area (*Image Source*), this allows the use of the active pattern shown in the Toolbox as a source.

Alignment

Determines if the source and destination stay in relation (*Aligned*) or if the source is reset to the originally indicated position when the mouse button is released (*Non-Aligned*). *Registered Alignment* makes sense only when cloning from another image. This will make the clone tool use the same coordinates for the source image and the destination image.

 ## Convolver (V)

Depending on the options set, this tool can either *Blur* or *Sharpen* images. To sharpen larger image areas or an entire image, use the *Sharpen* or *Unsharp Mask* filters (*<Image>Filters→Enhance*).

Rate

Determines the strength of the effect.

Convolve Type

This sets the effect of the Convolver (*Blur* or *Sharpen*). The setting can be toggled using the CTRL key.

 Ink Tool (K)

The ink tool is the only drawing tool that does not use the brush selected in the Brush dialog. Instead, the form and size of the Ink tool's brush is set in the Options window, which can be accessed by double-clicking on the Ink tool icon in the Toolbox. This tool was specifically developed for use with a graphics tablet, where the pressure and angle of the pen, as well as the pen's speed, determine how ink is applied to an image.

Adjustment

Specifies size and orientation of the brush.

Sensitivity

Determines how much the pen's pressure influences the brush size and how the tile affects the brush shape. You can regulate how much the brush gets smaller if the pen is moved very quickly.

Type

Selects one of several different basic brush shapes.

Shape

Allows you to modify the brush shape by elongating it in a specific direction by dragging the mouse.

 Dodge or Burn (SHIFT-D)

This tool simulates darkroom photo development techniques. *Dodge* will darken the image parts that it passes

---

over, while *Burn* will make them brighter. These effects do not use the current foreground color.

Exposure
Sets the strength of the effect.

Type
Selects one of two effects: *Dodge* or *Burn.*

Mode
Determines on what image parts the effect will be more pronounced.

 Smudge Tool (SHIFT-S)

Smudge simulates the smearing of wet paint. The brush will pick up some of the color that it passes over and will paint with it for a little while.

Rate
Determines how long the chosen color remains in the brush.

 Measure Tool

A tool that measures the distances and angles between points in the image. To measure the distance between two points, simply click on one and drag the mouse to the other—the distance is shown in the status bar at the bottom of the image. The points can be repositioned after they have been set. Pressing CTRL while dragging will force all movement to be horizontal, while pressing ALT constrains movement to vertical. Clicking on a set point while pressing SHIFT enables you to set another point by dragging the mouse to its position; the angle between the two connecting lines is shown as well.

The CTRL and ALT keys will place horizontal and vertical guides, respectively, into the ending points. Guides can be placed with a high degree of precision this way (see *Move Tool*).

Use Info Window

Opens a window that displays the distance and angle between the points and connecting lines just like the status bar does.

Color Selection

The current foreground (top-left) and background (bottom-right) colors are shown in the Toolbox. Double-clicking the color panels will open the color selection dialog. Pressing X or clicking on the double arrow will exchange the two colors. Pressing D or clicking on the lower-left icon will reset the colors to the default colors (black and white). These color fields are also the source and destination for drag and drop operations, which enable you to drag a color to the color selection of a plug-in or script.

Four tabs in the dialog offer different ways to select a color:

GIMP

An area is shown in which two color channels can be altered. To the right, a third channel is modifiable. One of the checkboxes to the right controls the third channel. Any of the channels from RGB and HSV can be selected (see "Color Models").

Watercolor

Imitates the mixing of watercolors. You can take some color from the left field by clicking the left mouse button, right-clicking will release the selected color.

Triangle

Enables the selection of a color that comes close to the subjective color perception. Rotate the triangle to alter hue. The saturation and brightness can be selected from the triangle itself.

GTK

Displays the standard GTK Color Selection dialog, so this will be the same dialog that is used by plug-ins and scripts. Hue and saturation are set in the circle to the left, while brightness can be selected in the field to the right.

Brush, Pattern, and Gradient Display

These areas display the current active brush, pattern, and gradient. A selection dialog is invoked by clicking onto the corresponding field (see "Dialogs"). In addition, these areas are used as source and destination points for drag and drop operations.

The Image Window

Every open image has at least one Image window associated with it. To conserve screen space, only necessary things are attached to the windows. The triangle in the upper-left corner opens the context (*<Image>*) menu. This menu can also be opened at any time by clicking the right mouse button. Figure 2 points out the various elements of the Image window. The functions available in the *<Image>* menu are described below.

The rulers at the top and left of the image display the current cursor position. The exact position is also shown in the status bar. If the *Dot for Dot* option is turned on, the position is displayed in pixel coordinates, otherwise the coordinate units are real length units (e.g., inches or millimeters). The rules are also the source of guides. See "Move Tools" under *Section Tools* for details on how guides are created, positioned, and removed.

Depending on the tool currently selected, additional information is displayed in the status bar next to the cursor position. Operations that take more than a split second to complete create a progress bar on the right side of the status bar; a Cancel button may be used to abort the operation in progress.

The two buttons at the bottom left of the image window, right above the status bar, offer quick access to a selection

---

Figure 2. The Gimp's Image window and its features.

technique known as *Quick Mask*. When the button with the
red rectangle is pushed, a red mask is placed on top of the
image. Those parts of the image that are to be selected can
be cut from the mask, or marked with a bright color. Pushing the left button will create a selection by analyzing the
brightness values of the mask. Double-clicking one of the
two buttons will open a dialog, in which the opacity and
color of the mask may be changed. As can be seen with the
help of the Layers, Channels and Paths dialog, this technique works by using channels (see "Channels" in the
"Dialogs" section); the buttons only offer faster and easier
access to it.

When working with large images, or if the magnification of the view is set too high, the Image window may not be able to show the entire image. You can then move the visible area by dragging the image with the middle mouse button.* If you get lost, click on the cross at the lower-right corner of the Image window (below the right scrollbar). A pop-up window will appear, showing the entire image with a white-bordered box that shows the current image viewing area. You can reposition the visible part of the image by simply click-dragging the mouse around inside this pop-up window.

When working with the Gimp, you may have many windows and dialogs open. You can temporarily hide all but the Image windows by pressing TAB once. If TAB is used again, the Toolbox is shown; pressing TAB once more makes all windows reappear again.

The following sections describe all of the functions that can be accessed through the <Image> menu. (As mentioned earlier, the <Image> menu appears when pressing the right mouse button in an Image window, or when clicking on the Image menu button in the upper-left corner of the Image window.) Not all of these functions can be applied to all image types. If the type doesn't match, the related menu entry is grayed out and inaccessible. Most functions support the RBG mode (see Color Models), which makes it the best choice in most cases. Sometimes it's also necessary to add an Alpha Channel (*using* <Image> *ImageAlpha→Add Alpha Channel*).

---

* If your mouse has only two buttons, you should configure your X server so that pressing both buttons at the same time emulates the middle mouse button.

File

Each Image window has its own File menu. The functions listed here apply to the image from which the menu was invoked:

New (CTRL-N)

Creates a new image. The values for image type and size are copied from the image that invoked this function.

Open (CTRL-O)

Loads an image from disk. The Open dialog is described in detail in the description for the File menu in "The Toolbox" section.

Save (CTRL-S)

Saves the image to disk. The Gimp recognizes the image type by the file's extension. You can manually select a file type from the *Determine File Type* menu. Some image types are not supported by all file formats. This is especially true when it comes to images with layers, since very few formats can save and retain the layer's properties. The Gimp will inform the user of a potential problem and will offer to convert the image into a format supported by the desired file format. As all changes are preformed on a copy, the original will remain unchanged.

"File Formats," lists all valid file types and their properties. Only the Gimp's own *.xcf* file format will save all of the image's information, such as layers, channels, guides, etc.

The Gimp can compress your images automatically to save space by (if the *gzip* or *bzip2* programs are installed) adding a *.gz* or *.bz2* extension to the filename. This is recommended when using the *.xcf* image type, since this format does not contain any native compression. In some cases, the *.xjt* format can be of help.

Like the *.xcf* format, *.xjt* saves all layer and guide information, but compresses image data is using the (lossy) JPEG algorithm.

Save As

Like Save, except that you are asked for a filename, even if the image already has a valid filename. This function makes it possible to save the image with a different name or in a different file format by giving it a different name or extension, respectively.

Revert

Discards all changes to the image and reverts back to the status of the image when it was last saved.

Mail Image

A simple but practical plug-in, this option offers the ability to email an image directly from the Gimp. A filename has to be specified, so that the file format can be determined. A short message can also be attached to the mail. The *Mail Image* option requires that you have a working mail system on the local machine.

Print

In the Unix version, this plug-in uses print queues to print images. Not only can it use PostScript, but it can talk with many laser and inkjet printers directly. The host system has to offer a print queue, where the spooler is connected directly with the printer and is not linked with a filter. Normally, this queue is called *raw*. Direct drivers are faster and of better quality than the PostScript driver.

The Windows version of the Gimp has a plug-in that uses the system print drivers and offers access to all available printers.

The dialog offers image scaling and positioning as well as brightness adjustments. The default values are often good enough for most laser printers; however, inkjet printers may need a higher brightness value.

Close (CTRL-W)

Closes the image. If the image has not been saved since the last change, you will be asked whether you want to close the image without saving your changes.

Quit (CTRL-Q)

Quits the Gimp. If an image has not been saved since its last change, you will be asked whether you want to quit the Gimp without saving the changes.

Edit

The Edit menu contains the usual actions such as copy, cut and paste, as well as a set of other functions for image editing.

Undo (CTRL-Z)

This is the most important function of the Gimp; it allows you to undo your last action. The number of undo steps can be set as described in the "Preferences" section, and is limited only by the memory size of your machine (both real and virtual).

Almost all Gimp's functions can be undone, with the exception of most of the scripts. Since scripts usually combine a lot of work steps, they disable the undo function before starting their work. This means that the whole undo stack is lost, and the script effect itself cannot be undone.

Redo (CTRL-R)

Redoes the last undone step.

Cut (CTRL-X)

Deletes the active layer or an existing selection and saves its contents into a copy buffer.

Copy (CTRL-C)

Copies the contents of the active layer or an existing selection into a copy buffer.

Paste (CTRL-V)

Inserts the contents of the copy buffer into the image as a floating selection.

Paste Into

Inserts the contents of the copy buffer into the image as a floating selection. If a selection exists, the contents of the copy buffer is inserted into it instead.

Paste as New

Creates a new image from the contents of the copy buffer.

Buffer

Provides these additional buffers:

Cut Named (SHIFT-CTRL-X)

Deletes the active layer or an existing selection, and copies its contents into a copy buffer labeled with a name for future use.

Copy Named (SHIFT-CTRL-C)

Copies the contents of the active layer or an existing selection into a copy buffer that is given a name for future use.

Paste Named (SHIFT-CTRL-V)

Opens a dialog listing all named copy buffers. You can select a copy buffer to insert into the image, or delete buffers that aren't needed.

Clear (CTRL-K)

Clears the contents of the active layer or selection, if one exists. If the given layer has an alpha channel, the layer is made transparent, otherwise it is set to the foreground color.

Fill with FG Color (CTRL-,)

Fills the active layer or an existing selection with the foreground color.

Fill with BG Color (CTRL-.)

Fills the active layer or an existing selection with the background color.

Stroke

Traces the outline of a selection with the current brush. This function offsets the lack of decent drawing tools a bit. In combination with the selection tools (see "Selection Tools"), it is possible to create geometric primitives.

Repeat and Duplicate 🐪

Generates multiple copies of the selection and pastes them into the same layer. The distance of the copies from the original can be specified.

Copy Visible

Copies the whole visible image into the copy buffer. Note that all layer information is lost—only the image as seen on screen is copied into the buffer as one single layer.

Select

The Select menu complements the selection tools (see the "Selection Tools" section) with functions to edit selections.

Invert (CTRL-I)

Inverts the selection. Everything that was not part of the selection is now part of it, and vice versa.

All (CTRL-A)

Selects the whole layer.

None (SHIFT-CTRL-A)

Cancels the selection.

Float (SHIFT-CTRL-L)

Turns an existing selection into a floating selection.

Feather (SHIFT-CTRL-F)

Fades the border of the selection. The width of the fading can be specified in pixels.

Sharpen (SHIFT-CTRL-H)

Removes the fading effect of a selection. The new border will be set to where the pixels were selected by 50 percent (i.e., where the border is displayed). Antialiasing of the selection mask will be lost by this as well.

Shrink

The selection will shrink by the number of pixels given in the dialog box.

Grow

The selection grows by the number of pixels given in the dialog box.

Border

Selects the border of an existing selection. The width of the border can be given in pixels.

Save to Channel

Allows a selection to be saved for later use. The selection is saved as a channel and will appear in the channel dialog (*<Image>Dialogs→Layers, Channels & Paths*). It can be converted back with the *CHANNEL TO SELECTION* command.

By Color

This function is a selection tool not present in the Toolbox. It selects all pixels of the same (or similar) color. It opens a dialog box from which the *Selection Mode* can be chosen. It determines how the new selection is combined with an existing selection. *Replace, Add, Subtract* and *Intersect* are offered as combination modes.

The *Fuzziness Threshold* determines how big a color difference between the selected pixel and a given color is allowed, so that both are considered the same. Select an image by clicking on it. This tools stays active until either a different tool is chosen or the dialog box is closed.

Round 🐫

Rounds the corners of a selection by a specified amount.

To Path
> Converts a selection to a Bezier curve, which can be edited with the path tool.

View

This menu gives you access to plug-ins that control display. These functions do not change the content of an image; they change only its display.

Zoom In (=)
> Zoom in one step.

Zoom Out (-)
> Zooms out one step.

Zoom (1)
> This menu lets you select a magnification in the range of 1:16 to 16:1, allowing you to give certain magnifications keyboard shortcuts. For example, the 1:1 magnification has a default shortcut of 1. See the section *"Creating and Editing Keyboard Shortcuts"* to learn how to create your own shortcuts.

Dot for Dot
> If this option is active and the current magnification is set to 1:1, each on-screen pixel represents a pixel in the image. This mode is very useful when creating or editing icons or web graphics.
>
> On the other hand, if you are editing an image that is to be printed, the real dimensions of the image are more important, and this function should be deactivated. The Gimp will display the image as it will be printed using the image's and screen resolutions. The resolution and the unit used for displaying the cursor position (e.g., inches or millimeters) can be changed with the *<Image> Image→Scale Image* function. To obtain an exact representation of the image, the screen resolution has to be set correctly in the *Preferences* menu (see the "Preferences" section).

Info Window (SHIFT-CTRL-I)

This window displays the following image information: size in pixel and the real dimensions, image resolution, current magnification, and image type and screen resolution.

Nav. Window (SHIFT-CTRL-N)

Shows a small version of the image, in which the currently visible part is marked. This section can be moved by dragging it with the mouse. Faster access to this function is offered by the icon at the bottom right of every Image window.

Toggle Selection (CTRL-T)

This toggles the visibility of the selection and layer borders. This action is useful if you want to look at an image without distracting lines.

Toggle Rulers (SHIFT-CTRL-R)

Toggles the visibility of the rulers. The unit used by the rulers is either pixels, or, if *Dot for Dot* is deactivated, the real-world unit that is used for the current image is used.

Toggle Statusbar (SHIFT-CTRL-S)

Toggles the status bar visibility in the Image window.

Toggle Guides (SHIFT-CTRL-T)

Toggles the visibility of the guides.

Snap to Guides

Aligning layers with guides is made easier by making the guides magnetic.

New View

Opens a new window showing the same image. Any number of views can be in use. This is mostly used to have a working window with a high magnification setting and a window in which the entire image can be seen.

Shrink Wrap (CTRL-E)

Adjusts the window to fit the image, if possible. Enabling the zoom tool option *Allow Window Resizing* will call this function automatically each time the zoom level changes.

Image

This menu offers functions to modify colors, perform image transformations which complement those in the Toolbox (see the *Transform Tool* section), and change the image type.

Mode

The Gimp uses different image types, each of which can display a different number of colors. With the functions in this menu, an image can be converted from one image type to another. Additional information about the image types can be found in "File Formats."

RGB (ALT-R)

Converts an image to the RGB (red, green, blue) color model. Since most filters and scripts work only in this color mode, this image type offers the greatest flexibility.

Grayscale (ALT-G)

Converts an image to grayscale, displaying up to 256 distinct shades of gray.

Indexed (ALT-I)

Converts an image to the indexed format. This mode uses a palette with a given number of colors. If no color number is given, a maximum of 256 colors is used. Only those colors that are in the image will be used if the *Remove Unused Colors From Final Palette* option is activated, or if a smaller color palette is needed. The dialog also offers the *WWW Optimized Palette*, which can be used to select the 216-color "web safe palette" that the converted image will use.

Reducing the number of colors will result in color banding in gradients. Banding can be lessened to a certain degree by selecting the *Dithering* option. If the file is saved in the GIF file format, Dithering will increase the file size. The following *Dithering* algorithms may be used:

Positioned color dithering
Well-suited for animations, since, in contrast to Floyd-Steinberg dithering, no flickering will occur.

Floyd-Steinberg color dithering (reduced color bleeding)
Under certain circumstances, this algorithm may produce better results than normal Floyd-Steinberg dithering.

Floyd-Steinberg color dithering (normal)
This option offers optimal dithering for most images.

Since the GIF file format has only a one-bit alpha channel, pixels are either fully transparent or fully opaque. To create the impression that pixels are semi-transparent, use the *Enable Dithering of Transparency* option. Better results are attainable with the *Semi-Flatten* plug-in (see *Colors*), which you can use just before the image is converted into the indexed format.

The Gimp offers only limited indexed support (many plug-ins operate on only RGB images). Generally, it is recommended to convert to RGB after loading an indexed file like a GIF; then do your work in RGB mode and convert the image to indexed just before saving.

Compose
Composes a color image from a set of grayscale images, one grayscale image for each channel of the resulting RGB image. Depending on the color model used (see *Color Mode*), you may need up to four grayscale images. These have to be the same size, but can be layers of a single image.

Decompose

Creates grayscale images from a color image. In the RGB color space, the resulting images are equal to those found in the channel dialog (see "Layers"). Using the CMYK model, you can perform a color separation for professional printing. However, professional printers with calibrated software and hardware will get much better results.

Colors

These functions manipulate the colors of the active layer:

Color Balance

This allows for controlled color shifting. Three controls that correspond to the three prime colors (RGB) and their complements are used to add and subtract hues. The effect can be applied separately on *Shadows*, *Midtones*, and *Highlights* by clicking on the corresponding button. Using the *Preserve Luminosity* option will prevent the color shift pixel intensity values from changing.

Hue-Saturation

Manages the *Hue*, *Luminosity*, and *Saturation* of the image. If the *Master* switch is enabled, the effect is applied on all hues in the same amount. For example, selecting a given hue enables you to transform all reds in an image to green.

Brightness-Contrast

This option allows you to change an image's brightness and contrast. Better results can usually be obtained with the *Levels* or *Curves* functions (both are in the same menu).

Threshold

Converts the image to pure black/white (i.e., not grayscale). A value histogram is shown, in which you can select values to be transformed to white.

Levels

Levels let you remap the intensity values of an image. The dialog shows a value histogram with three triangular markers below it. The markers determine what value should be mapped to black, 50 percent gray, and white. The corresponding values are shown at the top as *Input Values*. The middle field is the gamma value and is derived from the position of the gray triangle. The output values can be modified as well. This is done in the lower half of the dialog.

The levels are not only applicable to the values, but to any color channel, including the alpha channel. The appropriate channel can be selected from the menu at the top of the dialog.

Curves

Just like Levels, Curves remaps the intensity values of the image. The values of the horizontal axis are mapped to the values on the vertical axis. For a better orientation, you can click in the image, and the brightness of the selected pixel will be shown on the horizontal axis. The mapping itself is shown in the small bar below the curve. You can change the curve by dragging the control markers. To insert a new marker, just click on the curve. To delete a marker, drag it onto another. This tool also has a freehand mode (*Curve Type: Free*), that does not use control markers.

Curves can be used to change not only the values of the image, but of each color channel as well, including the alpha channel. Select the channel to manipulate from the menu at the top.

Desaturate

Removes all colors from the image, resulting in a grayscale image that is still of the RGB type. You can continue using colors in the image afterward.

Invert

Inverts the colors in an image. Bright pixels turn dark and vice versa, and all hues are replaced with their complements.

Posterize

Reduces the amount of colors used. The *Levels* control determines how many values each color channel is reduced to. Smooth color gradients turn into bands of the same color.

Auto

These functions automatically enhance the colors and contrast of an image:

Equalize

This function modifies colors so that all intensity values have approximately the same frequency. The result has more contrast, but can also have severe color shifts. Obtain better results with *Stretch Contrast* and *Stretch HSV*.

Color Enhance

Creates a stronger color contrast by stretching the saturation of the image's colors so that the entire range possible is used. Hues are preserved.

Normalize

Another contrast-enhancing function. Unlike *Stretch Contrast*, this operation stretches all color channels by the same amount. This rules out the possibility of a color shift.

Stretch Contrast

This gives the image more contrast between color ranges. Since this operation is applied to each color channel individually, color shifts can occur.

Stretch HSV

This function enhances an image's contrast as well, but since it operates in the HSV color space (see "Color Models") color hues are preserved.

Colormap Rotation

This function can map entire color ranges into others. For example, *Colormap Rotation* can let you change the color of a piece of clothing in a photo without changing the other colors.

Filter Pack

A set of image manipulation filters unified in a very intuitive dialog. Groups previews of the image with small variations in hue, saturation, and brightness around a preview of the original. Clicking one of the previews moves it into the center of the group, making it easy to approach the desired effect step-by-step. To undo the last step, simply click on the preview opposite the last one selected.

Alpha

The alpha functions to manipulate an image's alpha channel:

Add Alpha Channel

Adds an alpha channel to an image. This is the same function as *<Image>Layers→Add Alpha Channel*.

Clear Alpha 🐫

If parts of an image are made transparent using the alpha channel, information about the image's content is still available and can be made visible again by using the Eraser's *Anti-Erase* function. This Perl script sets the color of all transparent areas to a fixed color. The *Clear Alpha* option, when combined with the compression levels of different file formats, helps to reduce the image's file size.

Threshold Alpha

Similar to *Threshold* (*<Image> Image→Colors→Threshold*) but applied to the alpha channel. All pixels with an alpha value below a given threshold will be made completely transparent; all pixels above the threshold will be opaque.

Transforms

These menu items transform images, by moving or rotating an image:

Offset (SHIFT-CTRL-O)

Moves the layer horizontally or vertically by a specified amount of pixels. Unlike the Move tool, the layer is cropped at the edge of an image. The *Wrap Around* option determines how to handle parts that are moved out of the image area. If active, the parts that are moved out of the image at one side are pushed into the image from the other side. The *Offset By (X/2), (Y/2)* function makes it easy to create tiling images, as the corners are moved to the image's center and can be matched easily.

Rotate

Rotates the whole image by multiples of 90 degrees. This function does not work with images that contain masks or channels. To rotate a single layer, use the *<Image>Layers→Rotate* function.

Autocrop

Automates the *Crop* function. This function analyzes all layers of the image and crops uniform colors (i.e., where an image is empty), making it fast and easy to crop the image to its minimal dimensions.

This plug-in will crop all layers, but looks at only the active layer to find out where to crop, which can result in loss of image information to the other layers.

Guillotine

Chops up the image along any guides that were set with the Move tool, creating a bunch of smaller images. This can be quite helpful when creating images that are to be displayed in HTML tables.

Zealous Crop

Just like the *Autocrop* function, *Zealous Crop* crops areas of the same color (i.e., empty spaces). The image is not only cropped at the edge, but, if possible, parts in the middle of the image are cropped as well. While this

---

plug-in operates on the entire image, it will only analyze the active layer to find out where to crop, which may result in losing picture elements.

Canvas Size

Resizes the image without scaling the contents. A layer that goes over the edges of the image will not be cropped. To do this, use the *Crop* tool (see the *Crop tool* section). *Resize* is used to enlarge an image so that layers that surpass the image size can fit.

If the *Constrain Ratio* option is active, the horizontal and vertical sizes are changed by the same relative amount, preserving the image's aspect ratio. For example, enter 2.0 to double the image size.

The lower part of the dialog allows you to reposition the image in its new dimensions. Use the *X* and *Y Offset* options for exact positioning.

Scale Image

Scales the image to a new size, and affects all layers and channels of the image. The size can be given directly as a pixel value, or as a factor in the *X* and *Y Offset* fields. For example, entering 0.5 in the *Y Offset* field will shrink the corresponding dimension of the image to half its current value. To scale a single layer only use the *Scale Layer* function in the Layers dialog (*<Image>Dialogs→Layers, Channels & Paths*).

The lower part of the dialog allows you to change the image resolution. However, this does not scale the content—it merely adjusts the printing size associated with the image.

Duplicate (CTRL-D)

Duplicates an entire image, including all layers, channels, paths, etc.

Histogram

Displays an intensity histogram of an image, as well as information about the area marked by the cursor.

Layers

With some exceptions, all functions of this menu are also available in the Layers dialog (*<Image>Dialogs→Layers, Channels & Paths*), which is described in the *Layers* section. Nonetheless, we will show you how to select and move layers with the *Stack* menu, without needing to open the layers dialog. These functions are also accessible through keyboard accelerators, making it faster to work with images that contain many layers.

Rotate
   Rotates the selected layer by multiples of 90 degrees. Theoretically, this could also be done by using the Transformation tool (see "Selection Tools"), but the algorithm used here is optimized for the 90 degrees steps, and works much faster than transform.

Center Layer 🐫
   Moves the current layer to the image's center.

Align Visible Layers
   With the help of this function, you can align all layers using different modes of alignment.

Tools

Gimp's tools can be easily reached by using the icons in the Toolbox. This menu exists solely to assign keyboard shortcuts to them (see *"Creating and Editing Keyboard Shortcuts"*).

Dialogs

Most of the Gimp's settings are modified through the dialogs in the *Dialog* menu. The changes are done immediately. Dialog windows can stay open while you work on an image. All of these dialogs are accessible via the Toolbox menu (*<Toolbox>File→Dialogs*) as well, with the exception of the *Undo History*, which is available only from the Image menu (*<Image>Dialogs→Undo History*).

Layers, Channels and Paths (CTRL-L)

The most powerful feature of the Gimp is its ability to add layers, channels and paths to an image. The Gimp's Layers, Channels & Paths dialog should always be open because you will find that you will be using the Layers dialog very often. A menu at the top of this dialog allows you to select one of the currently open images. The layers, channels and paths of the selected image are then displayed in the dialog. Pressing CTRL-L in an image will make the dialog display layers and channels for that particular image. Activating the *Auto* option causes the Gimp to follow the currently active image and update the Layers dialog accordingly. An image is made active when an operation is performed on it. For example, pressing the spacebar when an Image window has focus will cause this image to become the active image.

Layers The Layers page shows the layer hierarchy of your image. The name of the layer is also displayed to the right of the layer. The layer can be renamed by double-clicking on its name.

The bottom layer is called *Background* by default. The background layer cannot be raised if it does not have an alpha channel. By adding an alpha channel (*Add Alpha Channel*), the background layer is converted to a normal layer which can be moved up in the stack.

The way a layer's colors interact with the other layer's colors is set in the *Mode* menu. This is explained in "Drawing and Layer Modes." The *Keep Transparency* option determines if the layer's transparencies are preserved at all times. *Opacity* controls the layer's color's degree of transparency.

As long as no floating selection exists, clicking a layer will highlight it, indicating that it is now active. A floating selection is its own temporary layer that is always at the top of the layer hierarchy; it has its own icon, and is labeled *Floating Selection*. A floating selection is created when a normal selection is moved, text is inserted, or a normal selection is explicitly converted to a floating selection with the *<Image>Select→Float* command. A floating selection layer is linked to its original layer, but can be transformed into a layer of its own, deleted, or anchored (merged) with its original layer.

The Eye icon next to the layer indicates that the layer is visible; the layer's visibility can be toggled by clicking the eye. If SHIFT is held down while the eye is clicked, the visibility of all other layers are toggled simultaneously—an easy way to look at a layer by itself.

Layers can also be linked. A linked layer is indicated with a Cross icon next to the eye icon. All linked layers are moved together, so that the relative positions of the linked layers do not change.

Additional functions are needed when layer masks are defined. A layer mask adds another transparency channel to the image. The mask itself is a grayscale image of the same size as the layer. A black mask pixel means that the layer is completely transparent at that position, while white indicates complete opacity. Clicking the layer mask selects it for editing. The mask can then be manipulated just like a normal layer in the Image window. Pressing CTRL while clicking the mask deactivates its function. In this case, the mask gets a red border in the dialog. To see only the mask in the Image window, press ALT while selecting the mask. This mode is indicated by a green border in the dialog.

Clicking the right mouse button over the layer stack opens a menu with functions needed to manipulate layers. Some of the more frequently used functions are also accessible via the icons below the layer stack. These icons are also used as the destination for drag and drop operations. Depending on where a layer is dropped, one of the actions described in Table 3 is performed.

Table 3. Dragging and Dropping to an Icon in the Layer Window.

Where the Layer is Dropped	Result
Between layers	Layer is moved between the two layers
On the new layer icon	A new layer of the same size is created
On the copy layer icon	A copy of the layer is created
On the garbage can icon	The layer is deleted
On a different image window	A copy of the layer is inserted in this image
On the Toolbox	Generates a new image from a copy of that layer

 New Layer (CTRL-N)

Adds a new layer or converts a floating selection to a layer.

 Raise Layer (CTRL-F)

Moves the active layer one position up in the stack.

Shift+ *Layer to Top (SHIFT-CTRL-F)*

Moves the active layer to the very top of the layer stack. This function is also accessible by pressing SHIFT while clicking on the Raise icon.

 Lower Layer (CTRL-B)

Moves the active layer one position down in the stack.

Shift— *Layer to Bottom (SHIFT-CTRL-B)*

Moves the active layer to the very bottom of the layer stack. This function is also activated by pressing SHIFT while clicking the lower icon.

Duplicate Layer (CTRL-C)

Creates a copy of the active layer right above it.

Anchor Layer (CTRL-H)

Merges an existing floating selection with its associated layer.

Delete Layer (CTRL-X)

Deletes the active layer or the floating selection.

Layer Boundary Size (CTRL-R)

Corresponds to the image resizing function (*<Image>Image→Canvas Size*). Scales the layer canvas without scaling the layer content.

Layer to Image Size

Resizes the layer's canvas to fit the dimensions of the image without scaling the layers content.

Scale Layer (CTRL-S)

Corresponds to the image scaling function (*<Image>Image→Scale Image*).

Merge Visible Layers (CTRL-M)

Merges all visible layers into one.

Merge Down (SHIFT-CTRL-M)

Merges the current layer with the one immediately below it.

Flatten Image

Similar to *Merge Visible Layers*, this function merges all visible layers, but also removes all non-visible layers and transparencies as well. Transparent pixels will be merged with the current background color. The result is an image with only one layer and no alpha channel.

Add Layer Mask

Adds a layer mask to the active layer. The mask can be initialized as black (transparent), white (opaque), or it may correspond to the layer's alpha channel.

Apply Layer Mask
> Merges the layer's alpha channel with the mask (which is consequently removed).

Delete Layer Mask
> Discards the layer mask without applying it.

Mask to Selection
> Selects according to the layer's mask.

Add Alpha Channel
> Adds transparency capability to the current layer.

Alpha to Selection
> Selects according to the layer's transparency (alpha channel).

Edit Layer Attributes
> Opens a dialog box in which you can change the layer's name.

Channels. The Channels page displays the channels of an image. In the case of an RGB image type, the red, green, and blue color channels are found here. Indexed and gray-scale images will have only one channel. The channels activity status can be toggled by clicking it. Each channel can have its visibility toggled by clicking the Eye icon as well. All image modifications are performed only on active channels.

Selections that are converted to channels with the *<Image>Select→Save to Channel* function are added here as a gray-scale image, similar to a layer mask. This channel will allow you to edit selections. The order of channels is without importance. An active channel can be manipulated in the Image window, and is overlaid with a hue that represents the channel's transparency. Double-clicking the channel name will allow you to rename the channel and modify the channels hue and intensity. The *Channel to Selection* function converts a channel back to a selection. This method of creating a selection is known as creating a QuickMask. Two icons in the lower left of the Image window allow faster access to this technique (see "The Image Window").

New Channel (CTRL-N)
Creates a new channel.

Raise Channel (CTRL-F)
Raises the channel one position in the channel stack.

Lower Channel (CTRL-B)
Lowers the channel one position in the channel stack.

Duplicate Channel (CTRL-C)
Adds a duplicate of the channel one position above it.

Channel to Selection (CTRL-S)
Creates a selection that corresponds to the channel's intensity.

Shift—

Add to Selection
Adds the channel to an existing selection. This function is also activated by pressing SHIFT while clicking on the Channel to Selection icon.

Ctrl—

Subtract from Selection
Subtracts the channel from an existing selection. This function is also activated by pressing CTRL while clicking on the Channel to Selection icon.

Shift-
Ctrl—

Intersect with Selection
Intersects the channel with an existing selection. This function is also activated by pressing SHIFT and CTRL while clicking on the Channel to Selection icon.

Delete Channel (CTRL-X)
Deletes the channel.

Edit Channel Attributes
Opens a dialog box in which you can change the channel's name, color, and opacity.

Paths. Paths are Bezier curves that define a selection, and are created by the Bezier Selection tool (see "Selection Tools"). This dialog offers access to these paths created to date. At the top, you will find four buttons that represent the different path editing functions. They are as follows:

New Point
Clicking here adds a new control point to the path. This new point is connected to the final control point in the curve.

Add Point
Clicking here adds a new control point between two existing control points.

Delete Point
Clicking a control point with this tool deletes it from the curve.

Edit Point
This lets you edit the tangent of a curve at the control point. You can set the tangent on each side of the control point separately by holding down SHIFT while editing.

The list below the buttons contains the paths that can be edited. A path's name can be changed by double-clicking on it. Clicking the lock to the left of the preview will lock a path to the image, and transformation tools will affect the path as well as the image. Right-clicking a path opens a menu that offers more functions. Some of these can be invoked by clicking the icons at the bottom of the dialog. The functions offered include:

New Path (CTRL-N)
Creates a new, empty path.

Duplicate Path (CTRL-U)
Adds a copy of the current path to the list.

Path to Selection (CTRL-S)
Converts the path to a selection.

Selection to Path (CTRL-P)
Converts an existing selection into a path and adds this new path to the list.

Stroke Path (CTRL-T)
Traces the path with the current brush in the foreground color.

Delete Path (CTRL-X)
Deletes the current path.

Copy Path (CTRL-C)
Copies the current path into the copy buffer.

Paste Path (CTRL-V)
Pastes the path in the copy buffer into the current path. A path can be copied between images this way.

Import Path (CTRL-I)
Loads a previously exported path from a file.

Export Path (CTRL-E)
Saves the current path to a file.

Edit Path Attributes
Used to change the name of a path.

Tool Options

Opens the Options dialog of the current tool. The same can be done by double-clicking the corresponding tool icon in the Toolbox.

Brushes (SHIFT-CTRL-B)

This dialog displays the available brushes. In addition to these, simple round and elliptical brushes can be created in any size by pressing the *New* button. Generated brushes can also be edited later.

The size of a brush is shown together with its name at the top of the dialog. If a brush cannot be displayed in its original size, a small cross is displayed at the bottom right. Open a full-sized preview by clicking on a brush.

A red triangle at the bottom right of the preview indicates that a brush is a so-called *brush hose*. Brush hoses are sets of several different brushes; the actual brush used is either random or determined by the motion of the brush. Clicking on the preview of a brush hose will display all of the hose's available brushes in a small animation.

Painting with a brush is similar to stamping; the brush image is drawn equidistantly onto the canvas. If the brush is regular and the space between the images is small enough, the stamping is not noticeable. Irregular brushes and large spaces create unusual effects. The space size can be set with the *Spacing* option.

Depending on the *Paint Options* (see "Preferences"), the dialog may also contain the *Mode* and *Opacity* options, which are available for all drawing tools. The mode of the color application can be set in the *Mode* menu. These modes are the same as for layers, and are explained in detail in "Drawing and Layer Modes." *Opacity* determines the covering power of the brush.

Available brushes are collected from the system and from your personal brush directories (*~/.gimp-1.2/brushes*). Complex brushes can be created by saving an image in a valid GIMP brush format. Simple grayscale brush formats end in the *.gbr* extension. Brushes with colors have the *.gpb* extension, while brush hoses end in *.gih*. A hose can be created from an image whose different hose brushes of the hose are either on separate layers or aligned in a grid. Pressing the *Refresh* button will cause the Gimp to reread all brushes from the brush directories, updating the dialog as necessary. This way, brushes can be added without having to restart the Gimp.

Patterns (SHIFT-CTRL-P)

This dialog displays the patterns usable with the Bucket Fill and Clone tools (see the *Clone tool* section). Most of the patterns included in the Gimp package tile seamlessly, making it possible to fill any area without a visible pattern restart. Pattern name and size are shown at the top of the dialog. Clicking a pattern preview and holding the mouse button opens a larger preview window that will display the entire pattern.

A pattern can also be placed into an image by dragging it onto the image with the middle mouse button. This way, the bucket fill tool does not need to be activated. (If you're using a two-button mouse, you will need to click on the pattern using both mouse buttons to simulate using the middle button.)

Patterns are collected system-wide and from your private pattern directories (*~/.gimp-1.2/patterns*). New patterns can be added by placing an RGB image in the Gimp pattern format (ending with the extension *.pat*) into one of these directories. The *Refresh* function rereads the pattern directories so patterns can be added without having to restart the Gimp.

Gradients (CTRL-G)

The Gradient tool (see the *Blend* section) allows the use of one of the many gradients shipped with the Gimp. Clicking on a gradient in this dialog makes it the current active gradient, while double-clicking opens the gradient editor. The gradient editor allows you to create new gradients or edit or delete existing ones.

The lower part of the gradient editor shows the current active gradient. A gradient consists of several sections, whose left and right borders have a color and an alpha value. The sections are the parts between the black markers in the display. The color fades from the left to the right border colors. White markers define the middle of the color transition. To set a color from a gradient as the current fore- or background color, simply click on it with the left mouse button.

A small area below the preview offers access to the gradient editor's diverse functions. Clicking the left mouse button will select a segment; pressing SHIFT while clicking adds a new segment. Dragging the mouse also moves segments. If SHIFT is held down while dragging, the segment's contents will be stretched. The right mouse button opens a menu offering more functions to manipulate the gradient.

Gradients are collected from a system-wide directory as well as from your private gradient directory (*~/.gimp-1.2/ gradients*). System-wide gradients cannot be deleted or changed permanently by a normal (non-root) user. Using *Refresh Gradients* will make the original gradients reappear. New and copied gradients are automatically saved to the local gradient directory. The *Save as Povray* function saves the current gradient in a format that can be used by the ray-tracing program POV-Ray.

Palette (CTRL-P)

Palettes allow you to work on multiple images while making sure that the same colors are being used. The Palette dialog displays some predefined palettes on the *Select* page. The *Named Colors* palette contains the more important colors along with the names the X server uses for them. The *Web* and both *Visibone* palettes contain colors used in web browsers and on systems with an 8-bit color resolution in different perspectives.

After switching to the Palette page, the selected palette is magnified. Clicking on a color will make it the current fore- or background color. Simple color modifications can be performed here as well. Right-clicking opens a menu that contains functions for creating, editing, and removing colors. New colors can be added by drag and drop as well. Almost all color selectors in the Gimp can be the source of a drag and drop operation.

Additional functions for creating and editing palettes are offered in the Palette editor, which is invoked by pressing the *Edit* button. Palettes can be imported from an open image or a gradient by clicking on the *Import* button. If more than one is selected (you can use the SHIFT and CTRL buttons for this), the palettes can be merged using the *Merge* option.

All palettes are read from your personal Gimp directory (*~/.gimp-1.2/palettes*). When the Gimp is first launched by a user, the system-wide palettes will be copied into this directory, so all palettes can be edited (or removed) by the user.

Indexed Palette

This dialog offers access to the palette of an indexed image (see "Color Models"). A left mouse click sets that color as the foreground color; a right click opens a menu that contains a set of functions to manipulate the current palette. Palette modifications are made in real-time.

Input Devices

The Gimp supports input devices such as graphics tablets, as long as the X server supports these as well and if GTK+ is compiled with extended input support. If this is the case, the input devices are listed and can be configured in this dialog. All that really needs to be configured for tablet pens is if the tablet area is to be mapped across the entire screen or only onto the active window area.

Device Status

This dialog displays the current tool, foreground color, brush, pattern, and gradient. Basically, all of this information is already displayed in the Toolbox, but it gets more interesting when working with multiple input devices. If the devices have been configured the dialog will display this information for each device (see *Input Devices*). Parts of the device configurations can be copied to and from others by dragging and dropping the attribute that is to be copied. Multiple pens can be configured this way without having to change pens in the process. If the *Save Device Settings on Exit* option has been activated, the settings will be restored when the Gimp is restarted.

Document Index

This index shows a list of all images ever opened with the Gimp. This extends the functionality of the image history list in the Toolbox file menu.

Error Console

If the error console is open, all error messages that would normally have opened their own warning dialog are shown here.

Display Filters

Available filters can be selected from the list on the left and added to the list of active filters on the right. These filters simply influence the way images are displayed on-screen and can be used to calibrate your monitor. The only downside to this option is that there aren't very many filters available at this time.

Undo History

This dialog, which is available only from the Image menu (*<Image>Dialogs→Undo History*), shows a list containing recent changes that can still be undone. Clicking a preview will immediately return the image to its status previous to the indicated undo step. The number of undo steps can be set in the Preferences dialog (see "Preferences").

Filters

Most plug-ins reside in the Filters menu.

Repeat Last (ALT-F)

Invokes the last plug-in used, with the same settings as before.

Reshow Last (SHIFT-ALT-F)

Opens the configuration dialog of the plug-in last executed.

Apply Perl Expression 🐫

Allows the versatile Perl-hacker to apply functions of the Gimp's Perl-extensions directly to all layers of an image.

Filter all Layers

Lets you select a plug-in from a long list; this filter is then applied with fixed or variable settings on all layers of the image. This option is especially useful when working on animations.

Blur

Offers various blurring functions:

Blur
    The classic, blurs with a 3×3 pixel matrix size. It can be applied several times at once.

Gaussian Blur (IIR)
    Well-suited for big radii and smooth color transitions (scans or photos).

Gaussian Blur (RLE)

Performs well on images that have big areas of the same color (computer generated images).

Motion Blur

Emulates a motion blur by superimposing multiple copies of the image.

Pixelize

Pixelizes the image, making it look as if it were being viewed at a high magnification level.

Selective Gaussian Blur

Another Gaussian blurring filter. Unlike the others, this one won't blur neighboring pixels if they are very dissimilar; it instead preserves contrasts.

Tileable Blur

A script that helps with tile generation by tiling the image before the blur is applied, and removing the tiling effect afterwards.

Colors

Includes color functions that are not found in the *<Image>* *Image→Colors* menu:

Map

These filters can be used to map colors or whole color ranges on other colors:

Adjust FG-BG

Changes all pixels in the foreground color to black and all pixels in the background color to white.

Alien Map 1 and 2

Makes images colorful and unreal by applying color shifts.

Color Exchange

Replaces one color with another.

Color Range Mapping

Maps one whole color range to another.

Gradient Map
> Colors an image with the active gradient shown in the Toolbox. The color selected depends on the pixel's brightness.

Sample Colorize
> A nice plug-in that colors black and white photographs. Reference colors are chosen from a second (colored) image.

Border Average
> Sets the foreground color to the average of the colors along the image's borders.

Color to Alpha
> Makes all pixels with a given hue transparent in such a way that if a layer of the same color is put behind the image, the original image is recreated. This allows you to easily manipulate background colors in pictures that blend into a monotone background.

Colorify
> Creates a colored monochrome image, similar to a grayscaling.

Fire 🐪
> Generates a burning border around an image.

Hot
> Seeks and modifies colors that would cause problems during a conversion to the PAL or NTSC TV format.

Max RGB
> Finds the maximum value for each color channel of each pixel and sets the other color channels to zero.

Semi-Flatten
> Paints the current background color under all semi-transparent pixels. Since this format does not support semi-transparent pixels, *Semi-Flatten* is useful for creating GIF images. The background color of the web page

in question should be set as the Gimp's background col-
or before applying this filter.

Smooth Palette

Generates a new image that contains the colors of the
original, in a format suited for the *Flame* plug-in
(*<Image>Filters→Render→Nature*).

Value Invert

Inverts the image in the HSV color space while preserving hue and saturation.

Noise

Filters that generate pixel noise, including the following:

Ditherize 🐫

Reduces the image colors as if *<Image>Image→-
Mode→Indexed* has been applied, but without actually
converting the image to the indexed format.

Hurl

Adds randomly colored pixels.

Noisify

Adds a random noise to the image.

Pick

Replaces random pixels with a copy of their neighbor.

Scatter HSV

Scatters the colors in the HSV color space and creates
image noise.

Slur

Similar to *Pick*: replaces pixels with their neighbors.
However, the probability is higher that the pixel on top
will be chosen as the replacement, making it look as if
the image were melting.

Spread

Shifts random pixels by a given amount. Creates a
strange blurring effect.

Xach Vision 🐪

Lays a color filter and black lines over the image, emulating the way robots see their environment (at least that is what those who watch too much TV believe).

Edge Detect

These filters detect and emphasize edges in an image by analyzing the image's intensity distribution:

Edge

Displays the found edges in their original color on a black background.

Laplace

Colors edges according to the intensity shift on a black background.

Sobel

Similar to *Laplace*, except that the algorithm takes the direction of the edge into account and generates smoother, slightly wider lines.

Enhance

These functions enhance the quality of an image. They are useful for editing scanned images.

2×2 Contrast Enhance 🐪

Enhances contrast using a simple algorithm using a 2×2 kernel.

Deinterlace

Adds missing rows to an image from a video source by interpolating the existing rows.

Despeckle

Removes dust specks and small scratches from scanned images.

Destripe

Removes the vertical stripes that are created by some inexpensive scanners.

NL Filter

A port of the *pnmnlfilt* program from the *pnm* package. This very versatile plug-in offers a set of nonlinear algorithms used to smooth an image, remove pixel errors, and accentuate edges.

Sharpen

Enhances the sharpness of an image. Most of the time, the *Unsharp Mask* filter produces better results.

Unsharp Mask

Overlays an image with two masks that were created by blurring the original image. As strange as it may seem, this approach leads to a sharper image, and unlike *Sharpen*, produces very few artifacts.

Warp Sharp 🐫

Another approach to enhancing an image's sharpness. The algorithm used here often gives even better results than *Unsharp Mask*.

Generic

Generic filters can be used in many different ways. They include:

Convolution Matrix

Allows you to manipulate an image with a freely definable 5 × 5 matrix. Blurring and shifting effects can be achieved this way.

Glass Effects

These plug-ins simulate the effects of light falling through glass:

Apply Lens

Shows the image as if it were being looked at through a round lens.

Glass Tile

Generates the impression that the image is being viewed through convex glass tiles.

Light Effects

These filters simulate light effects:

Flare FX

Simulates a lens flare, as if the sun were shining into a camera lens.

GFlare

Creates lens reflections, as does *Flare FX*, but offers more configuration settings.

Lighting Effects

A complex filter that emulates different lighting and surface effects. Grayscale images of the same size can be used as bump maps, RBG images as environment maps, etc.

Sparkle

Makes bright areas brighter and adds sparkles to them. This effect is obtained in photography by using an effect filter.

SuperNova

An explosion of light. Many of the parameters, such as color and position, can be modified.

Distorts

These functions move pixels around in the image:

Blinds

Generates the effect of open or closed blinds which are attached to the image.

CurveBend

Bends the current selection or layer along a definable curve.

Emboss

Creates a grayscale relief of the original. You could also keep your colors, in which case the effect would be like a *Bump Map* (*<Image>Filters→Map*).

Engrave

Creates a striped pattern. The thickness of a stripe represents the intensity of the original at that position.

Iwarp

Modifies an image in the preview with the mouse, after which the modifications are applied to the image. It is also possible to create an animation of the warping effect.

Mirror Split 🐪

Splits the image along the middle and replaces one half by the mirror image of the other.

Newsprint

Simulates the rastering of newspapers.

Pagecurl

Looks like someone is turning the page.

Polar Coords

Transforms the image from rectangular (Cartesian) to polar coordinates and vice versa.

Ripple

Moves pixels according to the selected wave form, similar to a flag rippling in the wind.

Scratches 🐪

Creates the effect of brushed metal by adding a lot of parallel scratches to the image. Looks good on metallic or grayscale gradients.

Shift

Shifts pixels horizontally or vertically by a random amount.

Value Propagate
Shifts and emphasizes pixels according to their intensity.

Video
Creates the impression of watching a television with bad reception.

Waves
Projects an image onto a rippled water surface, similar to what you might see if someone were to throw a stone into a pond.

Whirl and Pinch
Whirls and pinches an image.

Wind
Generates a comic-style wind effect by horizontally blurring the edges of an image.

Windify 🐫
Blows pixels around.

Artistic

These effects simulate classical painting styles:

Apply Canvas
Makes the image look like it has been painted on a rough canvas.

Cubism
Replaces the image with small, semi-transparent squares that are aligned and colored to approximate the original.

GIMPressionist
Repaints the image with the current brush. Size and form of the brush, the painting style, canvas surface—just about anything—can be configured.

Oilify
Emulates an oil painting.

Map

These filters can be used to map an image to different surfaces:

Bump Map

Creates a three-dimensional effect by using the brightness of an image's pixels as height information, and shining a light at it from a given direction.

Displace

Moves an image's pixels by an amount that corresponds to the brightness of the *Displacement Maps* pixel at that position.

Fractal Trace

Transforms an image with the help of the Mandelbrot-fractal.

Illusion

An effect that places copies of the original in a circle around the center of the image, making it looks as if the image were being viewed through a kaleidoscope.

Image Tile 🐪

Creates a mosaic from a number of images that resemble the image from which the script was called. The mosaic images are taken from a specified list of directories.

Make Seamless

Makes an image tileable.

Map Object

Projects an image onto a sphere or plane. The orientation of the object, its surface, and the lighting can be changed in many ways.

Paper Tile

Cuts the image into many tiles, which are then moved around slightly.

Pixelmap 🐪

Applies Perl expressions directly to an image's pixel values.

Small Tiles

Replaces an original image with an array of small tiles of the original (though the original image size is not changed). Single tiles can be rotated.

Tile

Generates a larger image by creating an array of tiles of the original.

Van Gogh (LIC)

Depending on the image source (either noise or some actual image), this filter can be used either to create interesting textures or as a blurring operator.

Warp

This filter requires another image as a displacement matrix. Your image will be well-stirred afterwards.

Xach Blocks 🐪

Projects an image onto a surface that looks a bit like a Lego® block.

Xach Shadow 🐪

Reconstructs an image from small tiles that are applied in an interesting, three-dimensional effect.

Render

These filters render a new image. The layer that is active when these filters are invoked is usually overwritten, and is only used to define the image size and type. The Render filters include:

Clouds

Not really useful to simulate clouds in the sky. Instead, these effects are often used as a source for bump map effects:

Plasma
Renders colorful plasma clouds.

Solid Noise
Renders a grayscale image with the help of noise functions.

Nature
These options allow you to create natural-looking images:

Flame
A complicated plug-in that computes fractals which sometimes look like flames. The *Smooth Palette* plug-in (*<Image>Filters→Colors*) was written so that this filter would be able to use palettes.

IfsCompose
Computes a special kind of fractal, called Iterated Function System, that sometimes produces results that look like trees or bushes, but contains classics such as the Sierpinski-Triangle as well. The equation that was used to generate a specific image is saved when the image is saved in the *xcf* file format. This makes it possible to make changes on the image or to recompute the fractal in a different size later on.

Pattern
These plug-ins are used mainly to generate background patterns:

CML Explorer
Performs a complex routine of mathematical functions to generate psychedelic images, which sometimes look like curtains.

Checkerboard
Creates a checkerboard pattern.

Diffraction Patterns
Creates diffraction patterns that look like interference rings.

Fractal Explorer

Provides a fascinating journey into the world of fractals.

Grid

Draws a black grid on the image that can be used to align picture elements.

Jigsaw

Generates a puzzle that shows the original picture.

Maze

Creates a maze (with no guarantee that the maze is solvable).

Mosaic

Generates a mosaic depicting the original image.

Qbist

Generates an image with the help of genetic algorithms, resulting in something that at times looks like abstract art.

Add Dust 🐫

Adds dust specks to an image, as you might expect to see on old slides.

Add Glow 🐫

Lets objects on a transparent layer glow.

Brushed Metal 🐫

Creates a surface that looks like brushed metal.

Burst 🐫

Generates lines that merge in the center of the selected area.

Dynamic Text

An alternative to the standard text tool that allows multiple rows of text to be entered at once. Text can be aligned left, right, and centered. The plug-in can read the text from a text file, rotate the text, and do many other things. The most exciting feature of this plug-in is its ability to edit text after it has been rendered. To edit

---

text this way, simply invoke the plug-in while the corresponding text layer is active. The layer shouldn't have been manipulated since the text was first rendered; otherwise all changes will be lost.

Fit Text 🐫

This plug-in fills a selected layer—or, if no selection was given, the entire image—with text in the best possible way. Simply select a font and enter the text to be rendered.

Gfig

Almost an independent vector drawing program, *Gfig* offers a host of geometric primitives. Drawings can be saved and loaded as well. Pushing the *Paint* button will draw the current *Gfig* image with the active brush onto the image or layer.

Highlight Edges 🐫

Creates a simple, three-dimensional effect on layers with alpha transparency by making their edges darker on one side and brighter on the other.

Random Blends 🐫

Generates random gradients, which may result in interesting pictures.

Sinus

Uses a trigonometric function to create a smooth, two-colored, wavy colored transition.

Sphere Designer

This filter can be used to generate spheres, letting you assign different light sources, textures, and bump maps.

Stampify 🐫

Transforms the image into a postage stamp.

TeX String 🐫

Uses TEX and a couple of other utilities to give the Gimp the power of professional typesetting. Requires TEX to be installed on the system.

Terral Text 🐫

Renders text with an interesting three-dimensional effect.

Web

Here are some useful tools for creating web graphics:

Image Map

This plug-in helps you create image maps (images that have different links assigned to image areas).

Perl-o-tine 🐫

Cuts an image along existing guides, just like *Guillotine* (*<Image>Image→Transforms→Guillotine*). This plug-in saves the image fragments in a GIF file format and generates HTML code to reconstruct the original image into an HTML table.

Prepare for GIF 🐫

Helps create GIFs that fade smoothly into the background, like *Semi-Flatten* (*<Image>Filters→Colors→Semi-Flatten*).

Webify 🐫

Automates the steps necessary to create a GIF image for deployment on a web page.

Logulator 🐫

The *<Toolbox>Xtns→Script-Fu* menu contains many of scripts that generate logos. These can be used to apply effects not only to text, but to other aspects of an image as well. The active layer must have an alpha channel (i.e., transparency).

NOTE

Logulator might be removed from Gimp 1.2, and will most likely be replaced by the *Alpha to Logo* functions found in the *Script-Fu* menu. The decision to retain or remove Logulator from Gimp 1.2 has not been made as of this writing.

Animation

These plug-ins are designed for creating, editing, and playing animated GIFs, using the layers of an image as frames for the animation:

Animate Cells 🐪
> Merges every layer with the background layer. This can be helpful when creating animations that involve an object moving in front of a static background.

Animation Optimize
> Makes transparent the pixels that do not change from one frame to the next. This can significantly reduce filesize.

Animation Playback
> Plays animation, offering an easy way to test it for web page use. Remove the image or animation from the window by dragging it with the mouse, and place it anywhere on the screen.

Animation UnOptimize
> Undoes optimization by replacing transparent pixels in a frame with the color of a previous frame at that position.

BlowInOut 🐪
> Creates an animation that pushes the current layer in and out of the image quickly.

Combine

These functions combine multiple images:

Depth Merge
> Combines two images with the help of two other images, which are used as height maps. At each position, the pixel of the image whose height map is lower is placed into the combined image. All images have to be the same size.

Film
> Generates a simulated film strip image, in which each layer of the original image is in a separate film frame. All open images can be added to the film.

Toys

These plug-ins are useless effects that are more eye-candy than anything else:

The Egg
> The "Easter egg" of the Gimp. Hint: use the mouse buttons to change the effect.

Guides 🐫

The Perl scripts found in this section make it much easier to work with guides. To see how to use guides yourself, refer to the *Move* section.

Center Guide 🐫
> Generates two guides that cross in the middle of the image.

Guide Grid 🐫
> Creates a grid made up of equidistant guides.

Remove Guides 🐫
> Removes all guides from the image.

To Selection 🐫
> Selects the image areas below the existing guides. For example, using *<Image>Edit→Stroke* will trace the guides with the currently selected brush.

Video

The *Gimp Animation Plug-in* (GAP), consists of a set of functions that are useful for creating and editing animation. The basic idea is that, unlike GIF animations in which every frame is a layer of an image, each frame is saved as a numbered file on disk, and each frame can have any

---

number of layers. The main feature is: a plug-in can be applied with static or variable settings to all of the frames in an animation. The GAP functions include:

Encode

GAP cannot encode MPEG movies itself, but it can invoke the corresponding programs (*mpeg_encode* or *mpeg2encode*) with the correct parameters. The encoding programs have to be installed separately.

Goto

These functions are used to navigate the animation. The selected animation is then displayed in a window of the current animation. It would be wise to give some of these functions keyboard shortcuts (see *"Creating and Editing Keyboard Shortcuts"*).

Split Video to Frames

Generates frame files from a given movie file. The movie file format is limited to MPEG and requires the MPEG library, or the animation player *xanim* has to contain the optional export function.

Delete Frames

Removes a number of frames from the animation, beginning with the current frame.

Duplicate Frames

Copies frames. This can be used to generate the beginning frame set of an animation. Simply save an image as a file that ends with *_0001.xcf* and copy this frame as often as necessary.

Exchange Frames

Exchanges the current frame with another frame from the same animation.

Frames Convert

Converts all frames of animation to another file format. It might become necessary to convert the frames to the *xjt* file format to save disk space. *xjt* offers all the features of the *xcf* file format, with the exception that the image data is compressed with the JPEG algorithm. Repeated loading and saving *xjt* files can result in visible artifacts, so this is not something that's recommended.

Frames Crop

Crops all frames to one size.

Frames Flatten

Merges the layers in every frame into one layer per frame and removes the alpha channel.

Frames LayerDel

Removes a given layer from all frames.

Frames Modify

Allows the execution of layer functions such as copying, deleting, or merging on all layers of an animation that match a certain pattern (this could be all visible layers or whose name contains a particular word).

Frames Resize

Resizes all layers of animation without scaling the layer contents. This function corresponds to the *Resize* function.

Frames Scale

Scales all frames of animation, including their contents. Corresponds to the image scaling function.

Frames to Image

Creates an image file that contains every frame of a layer. This image can then be converted to an animated GIF.

Framesequence Shift

Moves a sequence of frames within the animation.

Move Path

Moves a layer across animation. Since the layer in question can be scaled while it is moved, this function can be used to create many simple animations, such as a bouncing ball, moving text, or an approaching spaceship.

Split Image to Frames
  Generates frames in GAP format from an image that contains frames as layers.

VCR Navigation
  A comfortable front-end to the navigation functions—it even allows some frame operations, such as copying or deleting frames.

Script-Fu

The scripts in this menu modify an existing image. Scripts that generate new images are found in the *Xtns* menu of the Toolbox (*<Toolbox>Xtns*). As stated in the *Undo* section, most Script-Fu functions cannot be undone.

Alchemy

Witchcraft with images:

Clothify
  Makes the image look like it has been painted on a piece of cloth.

Erase Every Other Row
  Does what it says; it deletes every other row of pixels from the image.

Predator
  According to certain action movies, aliens see our world like this.

Unsharp Mask
  Enhances an image's sharpness with the help of two masks, which are overlaid as layers.

Weave
  Makes an image look like it has been drawn on a piece of textile woven from thick strips of cloth.

Alpha to Logo

The *<Toolbox>Xtns→Script-Fu* menu contains scripts that can be used to generate logos. The scripts found here can be used to apply those effects not only on text, but also on an image's alpha channel.

Animators

These scripts generate animation and are optimized for creating animated GIFs:

Blend
Blends two or more layers with a background layer.

Rippling
Makes an image ripple like a flag.

Selection to AnimImage
Creates copies of the current selection, applies a given plug-in with static or variable settings, and generates an animation.

Spinning Globe
Projects an image onto a spinning globe.

Waves
Uses the *Waves* plug-in (*<Image>Filters→Distorts*) to generate waves, as if someone threw a stone into a body of water.

Decor

These scripts decorate images with nice effects:

Add Bevel
Draws a three-dimensional frame around an image or an existing selection.

Add Border
Adds a colored three-dimensional border to an image.

Coffee Stain
Adds a coffee stain effect to an image.

Fuzzy Border
Makes an image fade smoothly to the background color at the edges.

Old Photo
Makes an image look like an old, faded photo.

Round Corners
Rounds the corners of an image and optionally adds a shadow behind it.

Slide
Adds a frame that looks like a piece of film to an image.

Render

These scripts can be used to render an existing image into the following visual effects:

Circuit
Looks like the blueprints of a circuit board.

Lava
Creates the effect of magma glowing through cracks in dark lava.

Line Nova
Draws lines from the center of the image to the edges of the current foreground color.

Make Grid System
Creates a grid system that will partition the image.

Selection

When used, the following scripts can be used to modify a selection:

Distress Selection
Disturbs a selection's borders, as if the selection were drawn with an unsteady hand. Selection size is not necessarily preserved.

Fade Outline
Softly fades an image within a selection.

Round

Rounds the corners of a selection.

To Brush

Creates a brush from the current selection and saves it in the brush directory.

To Image

Duplicates the contents of a selection to a new image.

Shadow

These functions apply different shadow effects to an image:

Drop Shadow

Gives the image or selection a shadow, to make it look as if it were floating over the background.

Perspective

Generates a perspective shadow.

Xach Effect

Adds a three-dimensional effect to an image or selection, as if a hole had been torn into the canvas.

Stencil Ops

These two scripts use grayscale images as a base for impressive effects:

Carve-It

Carves the grayscale image into any open image.

Chrome-It

Converts the grayscale image to a shiny chrome surface.

Utils

These utilities can be used to alter or view the composition of an image:

ASCII to Image Layer

Reads an ASCII text file and adds it as a new layer to an image.

Draw HSV Graph
Displays the HSV values of the image as a graph.

Show Image Structure
Shows the structure of the image (i.e., the layer composition), in a three-dimensional perspective.

Preferences

The Gimp has a variety of settings and extension possibilities. The configuration is saved in *rc*-files, which can be edited with any editor, such as *vi* or *Emacs*; however, many of the settings can be easily edited in the *Preferences* dialog, as found in the File menu of the Toolbox (*<Toolbox> File→Preferences*).

New File

These options allow you to specify attributes for new files that you create with the Gimp:

Default Image Size and Unit
Sets the default values for a new image, including the units used to display the cursor position in the lower right-hand corner. This is used only if the *Dot for Dot* option (*<Image>View*) has been deactivated.

Default Image Resolution
If the image is to be printed, it is recommended that you set this to the desired printer resolution. If it is a web graphic, you should set this to the screen resolution (72 dpi).

Default Image Type
Sets the default image type (grayscale, RGB, etc.) for a new image.

Maximum Image Size
To avoid a system crash due to lack of free memory, name maximum image dimensions here. The Gimp will warn you when a new image is created that surpasses this value.

Default Comment
>   Creates a comment to be saved in the image (supported in only some file formats).

Display

These options control how an image is displayed on-screen:

Transparency
>   Designates the size and color of the checks in the image display.

8-bit Display
>   On systems with only 256 colors, it may be a good idea to tell the Gimp to install its own colormap. Gimp will even refuse to start up if it cannot get enough colors when they are in use by other applications or a colorful desktop background. In this case, add the line (install-colormap) to your *gimprc* file (*~/.gimp/gimprc*).
>
>   An alternative to using marching ants to mark the border of a selection is to have the colors at the border change periodically. This can be used only on systems with 256 colors.

Interface

These options can be used to control the Gimp's user interface:

General
>   Sets the size of the previews in the Layers, Channels & Paths dialog and the Navigation windows as well as the file history list size.

Toolbox
>   Turns the current brush, pattern, and gradient displays on and off.

Dialog Behavior

Allows you to specify whether each image should have its own navigation window (*<Image>View→Nav. Window*), or whether the window display should be the active image. Likewise, it can be determined if the info window (*<Image>View→Info Windows*) should follow the mouse cursor, or if the information for multiple windows can be displayed at the same time.

Help System

Provides options for the Gimp's help system:

General

Tooltips and context help (see *Help*) can be turned off here.

Help Browser

Lets you use Netscape instead of the shipped help browser. The built-in help browser has the big advantage of being small and fast.

Image Window

The following options control the Image window:

Use Dot for Dot by default

It may make more sense to display images that are to be used as web graphics in a 1:1 ratio instead of using real-world unit length mapping. This option can be set individually for each image in the *<Image>View* menu. Only the default setting for new images is set here.

Resize window on zoom

Determines if the window is adjusted to fit the image after zooming.

Show Rulers and Statusbar

Turns off rulers and status bars in Image windows to save screen space.

Marching ants speed

Sets the speed of the dashed-line animation used to show the border of a selection.

Image Title Format

Sets the title of an Image window. Percent signs followed by a character have a special meaning, as shown in Table 4.

Table 4. Image Title Format Symbols

Special Character	Description
%f	Image filename
%F	Image filename, including full path
%p	Internal picture serial number
%i	Number of the image view
%t	Image type (RGB, indexed or grayscale)
%z	Zoom factor in percent
%%	Percent sign
%s	Images scaling factor
%d	Views scaling factor
%Dx	Displays an x if unsaved changes exist

Perfect-but-Slow Pointer Tracking

The Gimp may skip details in the mouse trail if the cursor is being moved too fast. This option prevents the loss of detail; however, the mouse cursor may fall behind the actual mouse movement.

Disable Cursor Updating

Prohibits tools from using their own cursor type.

Cursor Mode

Allows you to switch between different sets of cursors.

Tool Options

These options allow you to set preferences for the tools found in the Toolbox:

Paint Options

Settings like brush opacity can be set individually for each tool in the Tool Options menu, or globally in the Brush dialog.

Finding Contiguous Regions
>   Sets the default threshold for all tools used to select contiguous regions (for example, the magic wand).

Environment

These options help control things like how much memory the Gimp uses, and how images are saved:

Conservative Memory Usage
>   The Gimp will use memory more efficiently, at the cost of processing time.

Levels of Undo
>   The number of actions that can be undone. Note that enough memory should be available when this number is increased.

Tile Cache Size
>   Memory size that the Gimp uses to save image data. A swap file is used if more than this value is required. The value should be as large as possible on a single-user system, but not too high, as X and the Gimp core need some memory of their own. On a machine with 64 MB of RAM, a setting of 48 MB is recommended.

Number of Processors to Use
>   This option is available only if the Gimp has been compiled with multi-processing support. It sets the number of threads that can be simultaneously processed.

Scaling
>   Transformations can use different quality algorithms; better quality algorithms naturally take longer to complete. *Linear* is normally a good setting.

File Saving
>   The automatic generation of preview images when an image is saved can be suppressed with this setting. Also, you can determine if *<Image>File→Save* will always save the image in question, or only if the image actually has been changed after the last save.

Session

Window Positions
The Gimp can save the positions of most Dialog windows to *~/.gimp-1.2/sessionrc*, and can open these windows again at that position when the Gimp is relaunched.

Devices
Each input tool has its own active brush, colors, etc., which can be saved and reinstalled at the next startup.

Monitor

This monitor option controls settings for your monitor:

Get Monitor Resolution
To be able to display the image in the size of a printout, the Gimp has to know the screens' resolution. This can be obtained from the X server, although very few X servers return a correct value. A reliable way to determine the screen resolution would be to display a 500 × 500 pixel image with the *Dot for Dot* (*<Image>View*) option turned on, and measure the image's dimensions with a ruler. From the measured length, you can obtain the dpi resolution by dividing the image size in pixels by the image size in inches.

Directories

The following directories should be on the local hard disk, and not imported from other machines via NFS or other partition-sharing mechanisms:

Temp dir
The directory used for temporary files.

Swap dir
The directory used for the Gimp's swap files. As the swap files can be several hundred megabytes in size, it is recommended to use the system-wide /tmp directory.

The remaining items in this section are used to tell the Gimp where to look for brushes, generated brushes, patterns, palettes, gradients, plug-ins, and modules. You may specify multiple entries.

The rc-Files

The Gimp saves its settings in rc-files, which are usually located in the system-wide directories (*/usr/share/gimp* or */usr/local/share/gimp*) and in your personal GIMP directory (*~/.gimp-1.2*). Settings in your personal files supercede system-wide settings. Changes in these files will become effective after the Gimp has been restarted. rc-files include:

gimprc
> This file contains all settings for the "Preferences" dialog, as well as some seldom-needed functions that are not covered by the dialog. A well-commented *gimprc* file resides in the system-wide directory. Copy this into your personal directory and edit it to fit your own needs.

gtkrc
> Use this file to edit the GUI's appearance. Fonts and their size, background colors, and background images of the dialogs can be set here. the Gimp will read the settings from your *~/.gtkrc* file first. This file is used for all programs that use the GTK+ toolkit. Save any necessary special settings for the Gimp in *~/.gimp-1.2/gtkrc*.

ideas
> Contains a list of all images ever edited by the Gimp. This list is used for the Document Index dialog and for the file history in the *<Toolbox>File* menu.

menurc
> This file defines keyboard shortcuts for menu items. The shortcuts can be edited very comfortably in the Gimp (see the following section). The *ps-menurc* file in the system-wide directory can be used to install Photoshop-like shortcuts.

parasiterc

A parasite is arbitrary information attached to a particular image or globally to the Gimp. Parasites that are applied globally are stored in the *parasiterc* file.

pluginrc

A list of all installed plug-ins, which is generated automatically during the first start up. This file usually does not need to be edited. New plug-ins are added by copying them into a plug-in directory (e.g., *~/.gimp/plug-ins*). The Gimp automatically adds newly found plug-ins to this file.

printrc

The Print plug-in needs this file to store printer queue and user settings. The *printrc* file usually doesn't need editing.

sessionrc

If specified in the Preferences dialog, the positions of important dialog windows are saved here.

unitrc

Contains definitions of the length units used by the Gimp. New units can be defined in this file.

Creating and Editing Keyboard Shortcuts

All menu items in the Image and Toolbox menus can temporarily be given a keyboard shortcut. To create a shortcut, press the shortcut key combination while the menu item is being highlighted with the mouse cursor. Once set, the keyboard shortcut is visible and usable right away and continues to be available even after the Gimp has been restarted.

WARNING

The Gimp does not issue a warning if a previously defined keyboard shortcut gets reassigned. To reset the default settings, delete the *menurc* file in your personal GIMP directory.

Color Models

Different color models were mentioned in this book. A short explanation can be found here.

RGBA

This color model corresponds to the way colors are used by your screen. Colors are mixed *additively* from the prime colors red, green, and blue. Each color channel can have a value from 0 to 255. Therefore, 256^3 = 16.7 million colors can be used. There is also an alpha channel that defines the transparency of a pixel with values 0 (transparent) 255 (opaque) as well. The Gimp uses this color model in its internal color representation.

CMYK

The opposite of the additive RGBA color model is the subtractive CMYK color model, which uses the printing prime colors Cyan, Magenta, and Yellow to mix colors. Black is added to obtain a true black (the *K* in *CYMK* stands for *Key*). The Gimp's internals cannot handle this color model, but it is used in some dialogs.

HSV

This model describes colors with their hue, saturation, and intensity, and is very intuitive. The advantage of this color model is its ability to modify the hue of a color without having to adjust its luminosity, and vice versa.

The hues in this model are assigned positions on a circle's circumference and correspond to angles. Red is at 0 degrees, yellow at 60, green at 120, cyan at 180, blue at 240, and magenta at 300 degrees. Saturation values are in the range of 0 (gray) to 100 (saturated). Intensity values are in the same range.

Indexed

Some image file formats cannot handle the number of colors in the RGB model, and are able to select only up to 256 colors and write them into a palette. The colors are then referred to by their table index. The GIF image format is the most prominent example for this file type. The Gimp has only very limited support for indexed images, so it is recommended to convert an index image to the RGBA type directly after loading it, and then convert it back to indexed prior to saving.

Drawing and Layer Modes

The Gimp offers a couple of different color combination methods (e.g., colors on different layers). Sometimes there are no similarities to classical painting methods, so we will have to use a bit of math. Principally, the modes work in a way in which two colors are combined to create a third. Most modes use each color channel separately, except for the last four modes that work in the HSV color space.

Normal

Applies color to the background. If the color is totally opaque, the colors on the layers below cannot be seen. You can imagine your layers as a stack of slides, whose color contents is more or less opaque.

Dissolve

Makes some pixels opaque and some transparent. This mode works only on layers and brushes with some transparency.

Behind (for brushes only)

Applies color only where the layer is transparent, making it look as if you were painting behind the layer.

Multiply

Maps color channels to the value range from 0 to 1. Color channels of different layers are then multiplied, resulting in darker colors, similar to transparencies that are illuminated from behind. Adding color to the top layer makes the image darker.

Divide (Dodge)

Maps each color channel into the 0 to 1 value range. The colors are then divided to obtain the resulting color, which always creates a brighter color.

Screen

The opposite of *Multiply*. The mapped range is inverted, then multiplied and inverted back again, resulting in brighter colors.

Overlay

A combination of *Multiply* and *Screen*. Bright colors are made brighter while dark colors are made darker.

Difference

Subtracts the greater color value from the lower. White pixels invert the pixels below them, while black pixels will not change the color of the pixel below them.

Addition

Adds color channel values. Results greater than 255 are rounded down to 255.

Subtract

Subtracts the color channel value. Results smaller than 0 are rounded up to 0.

Darken only

Takes the smaller of the two color values.

Lighten only

Takes the greater of the two color values.

Hue

Replaces the lower layer's color hue with the top layer's hues while preserving saturation and intensity.

Saturation

Replaces the bottom layer's saturation with the top color's saturation, while preserving hue and intensity.

Color

Replaces the bottom layer's hue and saturation with the top color's saturation, while preserving intensity.

Value

Replaces the bottom layer's intensity with the top layer's intensity, while preserving hue and saturation.

File Formats

Different file format's loading and saving routines are actually plug-ins (with the exception of the *XCF* file format). This eases the addition of new file types. Table 5 lists the formats that are a part of the Gimp's standard distribution. Some of the plug-ins use libraries that are not part of the Gimp's distribution. If these libraries are not installed on the host system, the corresponding file type cannot be used.

Table 5. Standard file formats supported by the Gimp

Format	Extension	Saving	Loading	RGB	Grayscale	Indexed	Alpha	Layers
AVI (uncompressed)	*avi*	✓	✓	✓			✓	✓
Windows Bitmap	*bmp*	✓	✓	✓	✓	✓		
C Source	*c*	✓		✓			✓	
KISS CEL	*cel*	✓	✓			✓	✓	
Flexible Image Transport System	*fit, fits*	✓	✓	✓	✓	✓		
FLI Movie	*fli*		✓		✓	✓		✓

Table 5. Standard file formats supported by the Gimp (continued)

Format	Extension	Saving	Loading	RGB	Grayscale	Indexed	Alpha	Layers
Fax G3	g3		✓		✓			
GIMP Brush	gbr	✓	✓		✓			
Graphics Interchange Format	gif	✓	✓		✓	✓	✓	
Gimp Image Hose	gih	✓	✓	✓			✓	✓
Gimp Pixmap Brush	gpb	✓	✓	✓			✓	
C Header	h	✓			✓		✓	
HRZ	hrz	✓	✓	✓	✓	✓	✓	
HTML	html, htm	✓		✓	✓		✓	
SUN Rasterfile	im1, im8, im24, im32	✓	✓	✓	✓	✓	✓	
Joint Photographics Expert Group	jpg, jpeg	✓	✓	✓	✓			
Motion Picture Expert Group	mpg, mpeg		✓	✓	✓			✓
Gimp Pattern	pat	✓	✓	✓	✓			
ZSoft PCX	pcx	✓	✓	✓	✓	✓		
Portable Document Format	pdf		✓	✓	✓	✓		
Alias/Wavefront PIX	pix, matte, mask, alpha, als	✓	✓	✓	✓			
Portable Network Graphic	png	✓	✓	✓	✓	✓	✓	
Portable Anymap	pnm, ppm, pgm, pbm	✓	✓	✓	✓	✓		
PostScript	ps, eps	✓	✓	✓	✓	✓		
Photoshop	psd		✓	✓	✓	✓	✓	✓

Table 5. Standard file formats supported by the Gimp (continued)

Format	Extension	Saving	Loading	RGB	Grayscale	Indexed	Alpha	Layers
Irix RBG	*rgb, bw, sgi, icon*	✓	✓	✓	✓		✓	
Microeyes SNP	*snp*		✓			✓		
Truevision Targa	*tga*	✓	✓	✓	✓	✓	✓	
Tagged Image File Format	*tiff, tif*	✓	✓	✓	✓		✓	
X10/X11 Bitmap	*xbm*	✓	✓			✓		
Gimp XCF	*xcf*	✓	✓	✓	✓	✓	✓	✓
Gimp XJT	*xjt*	✓	✓	✓	✓	✓	✓	✓
X Pixmap	*xpm*	✓	✓	✓	✓	✓	✓	
X Window Dump	*xwd*	✓	✓	✓	✓	✓		

The *AVI, FLI* and *MPG* formats contain animation. This is also partially true for the *GIF* format, which can contain a still image as well as animation. The Gimp makes each layer of an image a frame in the animation. Only the GIF format can save an animation stack. The names of the layers are used to find animation information. The duration of a frame can be given in the layer's name. For example, an entry of "500ms" will display this animation frame for half a second before the next frame is shown. With the "combine" and "replace" parameters, you can determine if the layer is combined with the existing image, or if the frame completely replaces the previous image.

Get even more for your money.

Join the O'Reilly Community, and register the O'Reilly books you own. It's free, and you'll get:

- $4.99 ebook upgrade offer
- 40% upgrade offer on O'Reilly print books
- Membership discounts on books and events
- Free lifetime updates to ebooks and videos
- Multiple ebook formats, DRM FREE
- Participation in the O'Reilly community
- Newsletters
- Account management
- 100% Satisfaction Guarantee

Registering your books is easy:
1. Go to: oreilly.com/go/register
2. Create an O'Reilly login.
3. Provide your address.
4. Register your books.

Note: English-language books only

To order books online:
oreilly.com/store

For questions about products or an order:
orders@oreilly.com

To sign up to get topic-specific email announcements and/or news about upcoming books, conferences, special offers, and new technologies:
elists@oreilly.com

For technical questions about book content:
booktech@oreilly.com

To submit new book proposals to our editors:
proposals@oreilly.com

O'Reilly books are available in multiple DRM-free ebook formats. For more information:
oreilly.com/ebooks

O'REILLY®

Spreading the knowledge of innovators   oreilly.com

Made in the USA
Lexington, KY
15 January 2012